Card Games
for Two

Card Games
for Two

114346

SEAN CALLERY

WARD LOCK

A WARD LOCK BOOK

This edition published in the UK in 1994 by Ward Lock
Wellington House, 125 Strand, London WC2R 0BB

A Cassell Imprint

Reprinted 1994, 1995

© Text and illustrations Ward Lock 1994

This book was previously published in 1990

Distributed in the United States
by Sterling Publishing Co., Inc.
387 Park Avenue South, New York, NY 10016-8810

Distributed in Australia
by Capricorn Link (Australia) Pty Ltd
2/13 Carrington Road, Castle Hill, NSW 2154

British Library Cataloguing-in-Publication Data
A catalogue record for this book is available from the British Library

ISBN 0-7063-7223-9

Typeset by Columns of Reading

Printed and bound in Great Britain by
Biddles Ltd, Guildford and King's Lynn

Acknowledgements
Many thanks to A and C, Tim and Emma for their help in
researching this book and Jane Donovan for her help.

Cover photograph: Sue Atkinson. Picture courtesy of
The Picture Frame Workshop, St Leonard's Rd, Windsor.

CONTENTS

INTRODUCTION

Most people know something about cards and card games, but since this book aims to be suitable for everyone from beginner to enthusiast, the basic rules standard to all card games (unless indicated in the text) are as follows.

An ordinary deck has 52 cards, each in one of four suits – clubs, diamonds, hearts and spades. Within each suit, cards are ranked in value, from ace (high), then king, queen, jack, ten, nine, eight, seven, six, five, four, three, two. Sometimes the ace is ranked lowest of all, and when applicable this is indicated in the text. Some of the more complicated card games divert this set of values, turning, say, the jack or the eight into the top card in each suit or moving the ten up the ranks. In addition, some games use the joker, which is the most powerful card of all, beating everything.

These values are used to determine the winner of each trick – so that when one player leads a ten of hearts, he wins if his opponent plays the nine or below, and loses the trick if the jack or any other heart card above it is played.

In many games, one suit is designated as the trump suit. This makes it more valuable than any other suit, and when a player has run out of cards of a certain suit (called a 'void') which is led, he is allowed to play a trump card, and win the trick. The trump suit usually changes each time a new set of cards (hand) is dealt, commencing the next stage of the game.

Just about every card game begins with the pack being shuffled, or mixed, and then cut. Whoever did not shuffle the pack simply picks up about half the cards and stacks it under the others. Players sometimes 'cut' for the privilege of being the first dealer. Here the pack is spread evenly across the table, and each player takes one card. Whoever has the higher value card becomes dealer for the first hand, after which it alternates. Another way of choosing the first dealer is to deal the cards until one player receives a jack, and that player is then the dealer.

After the correct number of cards has been dealt to each player, in many games the next card in the pack is turned over to indicate the trump suit. The rest of the pack is turned face down in the centre of the table, and is called the 'stock'. When players replenish their hands during play, it is usually from this stock.

When a trick has been played out (in the case of all the games in this book, that means both players have put down a card) the winner usually picks up both cards, places them face down as a pair in front of him, and then leads for the next trick. The cards are kept so that the number of tricks won can be counted at the end of the game, and sometimes the cards themselves are examined as they can have scoring values.

In some of the games in this book, points are also scored by making 'melds'. A meld is a set of three or more cards, either of equal rank (a 'set', e.g. four sevens) or in sequence (consecutive numbers, sometimes same suit, others irrespective of suit). Once you have played the game a few times, you will soon learn the many types of meld and how they are collected.

There are a number of rules about how a player who makes a mistake in following the rules may be penalized. I have not included these in the descriptions of each game as this book is designed for those who play for fun, not for the determined gambler. However, common mistakes include:

Misdeals: Players end up with the wrong number of cards. If you are short of a card or two, draw cards from stock. If you have too many, hold up the cards so that the opponent cannot see them but can pull out the number required, and these are placed at the bottom of the stock.

Revokes: This is when a player plays an illegal card i.e. one he has no right to play. For example, if the rules are that you always follow the suit led, and you play a trump when you still have a card of the suit led, you have revoked. An agreed number of points is usually deducted from your score, and of course you are never allowed to win by playing an illegal card.

This book includes a number of gambling games. These should either be played with money of very low value (pennies are best) or with tokens such as counters, or matches. In a game between family or friends, it is not worth risking the ill-feeling of losing large amounts of money!

There are more than 100 card games in this book, including the variations. The book is divided into three sections, and as you progress through the book, you will find each section (or level) comprises games requiring a deeper understanding of how to play cards. Level one includes simple games that quite young children can play as an introduction to cards. Level two games call for some judgement and tactical knowledge. While some of the level three games are complex and will take some time to play out, calling for a fair amount of game strategy and a good memory for the cards that have been played through the game.

There are so many variations of card games that you should not be afraid to create your own special extra rules if you feel they will improve the game – provided both players understand and agree these rules before the cards are dealt! The golden rule is to enjoy discovering what cards you have in your hand and how they can best be used to defeat your opponent.

LEVEL ONE

BANKER AND BROKER (BLIND HOOKEY)

★ *OBJECTIVE:*   to have a higher value card than that of the banker.

Banker for this gambling game is chosen by cutting the pack, and during the game any player who has an ace with a bet on it becomes banker for the next play. (Tied players cut for bank).

The bottom card of the shuffled and cut pack is put to one side, and the remaining cards are cut into two 'piles' by the banker. His opponent places a bet on whether he will have the higher value card near his pile, and the banker then turns over his pile to show the bottom card. If it is an ace, he wins immediately. If not, he then turns over his opponent's pile, and whoever has the higher card value wins (banker always wins in a tie).

BEGGAR YOUR NEIGHBOUR (WAR)

★ *OBJECTIVE:*   to win all the cards.

Each player is dealt 26 cards. The object is to win all 52 cards. Each turns up his top card and places it in front of his pile. The higher card wins the other (ace ranks lowest), and the pair is placed face down by the winner. If both cards are the same rank, 'war' is declared. They are put in the centre with one further card each, and the winner of the next round wins all six cards. If ranks are equal for this round, the process is repeated. Although the aim is to win the whole deck, it is more usual to award the game to the first player to win three 'wars'.

Variation

★ *PERSIAN PASHA* In this variation, players turn up their cards one at a time in single piles, until two cards of the same suit appear in the same round. The higher card wins all the opposing turned up cards, which are kept separate from the hand. The game ends when a pair of the same suit cannot be matched, and the player with most cards wins.

BINGO

★ *OBJECTIVE:* to match cards in your hand with those turned up.

This game uses two ordinary decks with different backs. The dealer deals two hands of five, and the rest of that pack is dead. The hands are then turned face up in front of each player. Both put an agreed sum into the pot, and the dealer then turns the top card from the other deck face up, announcing its numerical value and suit. If either player has the same card, he turns it face down. Play continues until one hand is all faced down.

CONCENTRATION

★ *OBJECTIVE:* to collect all the cards.

This game is also known as Memory or Pelmanism. The shuffled 52-card deck is dealt face down in a number of rows, so that no cards overlap. An option is to use a smaller space and deliberately half overlap some cards, which makes the game harder!

Each player turns up a card, and the highest card is the winner. If both are of the same rank, another two cards are turned. The cards are then replaced in the same positions. Now the first player turns up two cards, one at a time, and if they form a pair (same rank), he puts them face down in front of himself and repeats the process. If the cards are not a pair, they are replaced and the next player takes a turn. The challenge is to remember the positions of the various replaced cards, so that you can make a pair if you happen to turn up a suitable card. When all pairs are collected, the player with the most wins.

Variation

★ When you have perfected this memory game, try turning up four cards at a turn to collect the whole set!

CRAZY EIGHTS

★ *OBJECTIVE:*   to get rid of all your cards.

Each player receives five cards, and eight are then placed face up in rows of four. The aim is to get rid of your hand my matching its cards with those in the centre.

Non-dealer starts by placing a card from his hand face up on one of matching rank in the centre. Play continues, and anyone unable to play says 'pass'. The winner is the person who empties his hand first, and shouts 'crazy eights'. If both players pass, neither can win outright and their hands are scored by face value, picture cards counting 10 and aces 15, others by face value. If a player won the round outright, he scores nothing and his opponent's hand is scored. The lowest score after an agreed number of rounds wins.

FAN-TAN (SEVENS)

★ *OBJECTIVE:*   to get rid of all your cards.

Ace counts low in this gambling game, which requires both players to put one or more tokens into a pool before starting. Each player is dealt one card at a time per round until the pack is exhausted. Non-dealer starts by laying any sevens in his hand face up in the centre of the table. If he has none, he passes.

Once the seven is down, players can put the card of the same suit immediately higher or lower in rank (in this case the eight or the six) above or below it. The game continues with each player putting down one card per round, of if they cannot play, putting one token into the pool. The first player to get rid of all his cards wins and takes the pot. His opponent must pay him one token for every card left in his hand.

Variations

★ *DOMINO FAN-TAN* Fan-Tan as described above can be played by up to eight players. This is a specifically two-handed variation. Each player is only dealt 17 cards, and the rest of the pack forms the stock. If a player cannot take his turn to play, he puts a token in the pot and draws the next card from stock. If he still cannot play, he repeats the process until he can put down a card.

★ *AROUND THE CORNER* In this variation play can begin with any card, not necessarily a seven, and the sequences must be added in ascending order. When a king is down, the ace and two are the next cards in the sequence (hence the game's name).

GO FISH

★ *OBJECTIVE:*   to collect all the cards in the pack.

Go Fish is a simple game which children as young as six can enjoy. Hands of seven cards are dealt, and the remainder of the pack placed in the centre of the table, forming the stock. The aim is to collect all the cards in the pack.

The non-dealer starts by asking his opponent to hand over all cards he holds of a specified rank. The player asking must have at least one card of the same rank. If his opponent has any such cards, he hands them over. If not, he says 'go fish', and the player picks up the top card from stock. If this card happens to be of the rank he requested, he shows it and takes another turn. If not, his opponent can ask for cards of a certain rank, and so play continues.

As soon as a player has all four cards of one rank, he places them in front of him. If this means he has no cards left in his hand, he takes a card from stock as his next turn. The winner is the player who gains most sets.

LAST CARD

★ *OBJECTIVE:*   to hold the last card in the game.

This game is so-called because whoever has the last card or cards wins. Two hands of ten are dealt, the next card being turned up to denote trumps. Starting with the non-dealer, tricks are then played for, although there is no obligation to follow suit or trump. The winner of each trick takes a card from stock, and leads for the next. Eventually one player will run out of cards: his opponent wins.

MAU-MAU

★ *OBJECTIVE:*   to get rid of all your cards.

Cards in Mau-Mau are valued as follows: jack 20, eight 20, seven and ace 15 each, queen and king 10 each, other cards by their face values. The object is to score 100 or more points (although some people go as high as 500) by getting rid of your hand and scoring points for the cards still held by your opponent. Whoever cuts the lowest from the pack is the first dealer, then it alternates.

Seven cards each are dealt one at a time. The top card of stock is placed face up as the start of the discard pile.

Play consists of discarding one upturned card at a time on the discard pile. It must match the previous discard in either suit or rank. If a player cannot discard, he picks up the top card from stock, and this completes his turn.

If an eight is discarded, the next player cannot discard but must pick up three cards from stock. If a player discards a jack, he is permitted to immediately discard a second jack. In addition, he may call a change of suit, which his opponent must follow. If the jack is discarded without a change of suit being called, the opponent does not have to follow suit or rank, and can discard any card.

If the previous discard is a jack, seven, or eight, and the player cannot follow suit, he can either discard at the same rank or take a card from stock and save these valuable cards for later tactical use.

When a player has only one card left, he must announce 'one card'. If he forgets, he cannot discard and must take a card from stock. Play ends when a player has no cards left. He scores the total points for the remaining cards held by his opponent. If the first card in the discard pile is a spade, his score is doubled. If the player who went out finished by discarding two jacks, his score is quadrupled.

Hands are played until someone reaches 100 points or more. The strategy of Mau-Mau is to try and play one's long suit, or any suit your opponent fails to respond to. Try to save sevens and eights so that they can be played consecutively near the end, increasing the size of your opponent's hand.

OLD MAID

★ **OBJECTIVE:**   to avoid being left with the last queen.

This game uses a 52-card deck, with the queen of clubs set aside. The remaining 51 cards are dealt (it does not matter that one player has more than the other). The aim is to get rid of all these cards by putting them into pairs of the same rank.

Each player spreads his cards turned up, placing any pairs face up in the centre of the table. The rest of each hand is then shuffled and whoever holds the unpaired third queen holds up his hidden hand for his opponent to draw a card from. The opponent makes any pairing, shuffles his hand and holds it up for the process to continue. Eventually all cards will be paired except for the queen ('old maid'), and whoever holds it loses the round. Play continues until a specified number of rounds (say, five) have been played.

OLD MAN'S BUNDLE

★ **OBJECTIVE:**   to gain as many cards as possible.

Each player is dealt four cards, and another four are placed face up on the table. Players receive another four cards each time the hands are played out, but no more are put in the centre.

The non-dealer leads first, then play alternates. He can either 'take in' a card from the table with a card of the same rank from the hand, or 'trail' by placing a card face up on the table. Cards 'taken in' are placed in a pile, face up. A player can obtain his opponent's bundle by taking it in with a card of the same rank as the top card. When the pack is exhausted, the player left holding the most cards wins.

PISHE PASHA

★ **OBJECTIVE:**   to get rid of all your cards.

This game uses two standard decks, and the aim is to get rid of all cards in your stock and discard pile by laying them off on the four foundation piles or your opponent's discard pile.

Foundations are provided by the four aces. As each

becomes available, it is placed in one of the reserved spaces between each player's stock and discard piles. Foundations are built up in a suit and sequence, and once played there, cards cannot be removed.

Each player receives 26 cards (a pair first, then in threes) and these form each player's stock. The non-dealer starts by turning up his top card. If it is an ace it is placed in one of the foundation's reserved spaces, and he turns up another card. When he cannot play, he discards, starting off his discard pile. The dealer then turns up his top card, and places it either on a foundation pile if it is the correct card, or on his opponent's discard pile if the card begins a descending or ascending sequence in rank (suits are irrelevant). He continues until he has to start his own discard pile, and play reverts to the non-dealer.

When stock is used up, the discard pile comes back into play as the new stock. Having played a card from stock, a player completes all possible moves before it is his opponent's turn. The game ends when a player places his last card, and calls 'game'. He scores one point for each card left in his opponent's stock and discard pile. The overall winner achieves a pre-set target, of, say, 100 points.

PONTOON

★ *OBJECTIVE:*   to build a hand scoring 21 points.

Players turn up one card at a time from the pack and the first to draw a jack becomes banker. He deals one card each, face down, and his opponent may examine his card.

The aim is to reach a total value of 21 (aces count 11 or 1 at the holder's discretion). He judges his changes of achieving this (an ace is an excellent start, middling cards like eights pretty poor) and bets accordingly before the next card is supplied. If he has an ace and a ten-count card (a pontoon) he exposes it. If he has two aces, he can split them and start two separate hands.

The non-dealer has three options. He can stick and receive no more cards (but must have a minimum of 15 points); he can buy a card by increasing (but not exceeding) his stake; or he can twist, asking the dealer to provide another card, face up, for no extra stake. If a player does not have a pontoon or a strong hand, like two tens (scoring 20) he will probably try for a five-card hand. This comprises five cards with a collective value no higher than 21. When he is satisfied with his hand, or has exceeded a 21 score (gone bust) the dealer takes his turn.

He exposes his cards and if he has a pontoon wins immediately. Otherwise he can stick, or twist, until he exceeds 21 or is happy with his hand. He cannot split his hand and play two. At this stage the opponent shows his cards, and whoever has the score nearest 21 wins,

CARDS CAN BE ANY SUIT.

PONTOON

FIVE CARD HAND

SCORE UNDER 15:
PLAYER MUST BUY OR TWIST

If you are dealt two cards of the same value, you can split them and play two hands

unless one player has a five-card trick, which beats anything except pontoon.

If the dealer wins, he takes in the stake money, if he loses, the opponent gets double his stake back, and if he loses to a pontoon, the dealer pays double the stake plus the original stake. A pontoon maker automatically becomes banker next turn.

Variations

★ A third special hand of three 7s beats everything and dealer has to pay three times the stake money.

Any pair, not just aces, can be split and played as two hands.

A particularly fair variation is for the dealer to examine his hand after the second deal, and expose a pontoon if he has one, preventing his opponent betting on a hopeless cause.

★ *QUINZE* This variation is specifically designed for two players, and the target number is 15, not 21. Ace always counts as one. Rules are as for pontoon, except both players put in stakes and one takes the winnings (or if there is a draw, the stakes for the next round are doubled), so there is no banker.

★ **THIRTY ONE** Again, there is no banker, but now aces count 11, and three cards are dealt, one at a time, with an additional hand of three placed face down in the centre. This extra hand is exposed, and one player (having won the pre-game cut for the privilege) has the first chance to exchange any of his cards for any on the table. His opponent can then do the same. This continues until one player is happy with his hand and knocks the table. He cannot do this directly after an exchange, but must wait for his next turn. After he has knocked, his opponent has one last chance to exchange a card, before both hands are exposed and the winner identified.

This time the aim is to score 31, but all in cards of the same suit. If no-one scores 31, the highest ranking trio of court cards wins, and after that, the highest total scored.

PUT AND TAKE

★ **OBJECTIVE:**   to hold cards which match a hand drawn from stock.

To start this gambling game, the dealer deals five cards to his opponent. He then deals himself one card face up. The other player must put one betting unit in the pot for every card in his hand which matches it in rank. The second card is dealt, and this time the bet must be of two units per card, the third card requires four units, the fourth eight, and the fifth card 16 units.

Banker now picks up his hand, places it face up on the bottom of the pack, and deals himself another five, face up, one at a time. This time, the process is reversed and his opponent removes from the pot the appropriate betting units for each card. Any units left in the pot go to the banker. If the pot owes money, the banker meets the debt.

RED DOG

★ *OBJECTIVE:*   to hold higher ranking cards than your opponent.

In this gambling game the aim is to hold in the hand a card of the same suit but higher in rank than a card dealt from the pack.

Dealer is the person who receives the first ace as the cards are being dealt. Then it alternates with every game. Five cards each are dealt face down one at a time. The non-dealer places his bet on whether he had a card to beat the top card of stock, and the top card from the pack is turned up. If he has a higher ranking card of the same suit, he wins the bet and gets twice his stake back. If not, his bet goes into the pot.

Variation

★ *SLIPPERY SAM (or Six Spot Red Dog)* Three cards each are dealt face down, and the dealer then turns one card face up in front of him. His opponent may bet up to the entire pot limit before looking at his cards, or he may refuse to bet against the banker's upturned card, and ask that this card be discarded and that the banker deals a second card face up from the top of the pack. For this privilege the player must put a previously agreed amount into the pot (usually a fifth of its sum total). He can do this up to three times. After this he can either bet or pass as in Red Dog.

SNAP

★ *OBJECTIVE:*   to collect the entire pack.

A great rowdy game and often the first card game people learn. Each player receives half the standard pack as his hand, which he keeps face down and cannot examine or shuffle. Play begins with the non-dealer placing a card face up on the table, and his opponent places another card directly on top of it. Play continues until a card is put down which is of the same rank as the previous card. First to say (or better, shout) 'Snap' picks up all the cards on the table, adds them to the bottom of his pile of cards, and commences play again, which continues until one player has all the cards in the pack.

YABLON (IN-BETWEEN OR ACE-DEUCE)

★ *OBJECTIVE:*   to hold a card valued between two cards face up.

Suits have no value in this betting game, in which the object is to be dealt a card whose rank will be between two cards previously dealt to that player – so the best hand is a two and an ace, as this has the largest gap in value. First, both players put tokens into a central pot.

The dealer is decided by dealing out cards until someone gets an ace – that person is the dealer. He deals two cards each, face down. The non-dealer looks at his hand and places a bet near the pot, according to how he rates his chances, and a third card is dealt to him, face up. He turns over his hand and if the card he was dealt is between his first two in value he gets his stake back. If he does not, his bet goes into the pot.

Play continues until the pot is taken, or the stakes get too high!

♠

LEVEL TWO

BEAT YOUR NEIGHBOUR (ROLLOVER)

★ *OBJECTIVE:*   to beat the card played by your opponent.

This gambling game is a variation of Seven Card Stud. Seven cards are dealt, face down, and both players gather them up into a pack, without looking at them. The non-dealer turns up one card and bets on whether he thinks it will be higher than his opponent's first card. The dealer then turns up his cards until he plays one which beats his opponent's card. If he does, he wins the stake and new hands are dealt. When either player runs out of cards without beating the other, he loses the stake.

BOURE (BOO-RAY)

★ *OBJECTIVE:*   to obtain a trick-winning hand.

Players put an agreed amount into the pot. Five cards are dealt to each person, the next card being turned up to denote trump. Either player can then throw in their hand or drop out of the game, or stay in and compete for the pot. If both stay in the game, either can then discard and draw up to four cards from stock, or stay as he is.

Tricks are then played out, and the leader for each must play his highest trump if he has the ace, king, or queen. The player taking the most tricks wins the pot.

CINCH

★ *OBJECTIVE:*   to build a trick-winning hand.

This uses a standard deck, with aces counting high, and the usual ranks with one exception. There is a trump suit, and the five of the suit of matching colour is also a trump, ranking above the four but below the five. So if clubs are trumps the five of spades is also a trump. Five of trumps is called 'Right Pedro' and its colour match is called 'Left Pedro'. Trump cards won in a trick score as follows:

Right Pedro	5
Left Pedro	5
Ace	1
Two	1
Jack	1
10	1

Thus 14 points can be won on each deal. Nine cards each are dealt, in threes. Each player then makes one bid, naming the number of points he will make (from 1 to 14), and his trump suit. Highest bid is accepted and the game begins.

Hands must now be reduced to six, so each player discards, face up, as many cards as he likes, and draws from stock the number required to bring his hand back to six if necessary. Because Cinch is basically a one-suit game (trumps) this is obviously the stage to try and improve the trump content of your hand.

Tricks are then played for, and the object is to win tricks containing the scoring cards. The highest bidder leads. Each player must follow suit unless he can trump.

After this stage, points are counted, and if the bidder made his contract (by equalling or exceeding his bid) he wins the difference between the two players' totals. If he fails to make his contract, his opponent scores his tricks plus the amount of the bid. First to 51 points is the winner.

COMET

★ **OBJECTIVE:**   to get rid of all your tricks.

This game is played alternating two unusual decks. Take two decks and remove all aces, then separate the pack into red and black cards. Finally, swap a red and a black nine over. The nine of the opposite colour in each pack is called the 'comet', and is used rather like a wild card. Suits are irrelevant.

Each player receives 18 cards in batches of three, and the remaining 12 are set aside. The aim of the game is to get rid of all these cards. Non-dealer starts by placing cards from his hand in ascending sequence in the centre of the table, announcing each number until he can add no more. The dealer has to continue the sequence. Play continues until one player is unable to add to the sequence, in which case he says 'pass'. His opponent then starts another pile, on top of the first. A king is always a stop in a sequence.

If a player holds four same-rank cards, or three 9s (with or without the comet), he can play them in one go. So he would announce '3, four 4s, 5, no 6', leaving his opponent to play a 6. The comet can be played as any rank and acts as a stop. A player cannot be forced to play it, even if it is his only playable card.

First to empty his hand scores the value of his opponent's hand, with court cards counting 10. The score is doubled if his opponent holds a comet, or if the winning player uses a comet as his last card. If he goes out by playing the comet as a nine, his score quadruples.

The best way to play Comet is to get rid of duplicated

cards first, and remember which cards acted as stops for your opponent.

COON CAN

★ **OBJECTIVE:**   to get rid of all cards by melding.

Using two full packs and two jokers, 10 cards are dealt to each player, the remainder forming the stock, with the top card turned over to start the discard pile.

Starting with the non-dealer, each player in turn draws a card from stock or the top of the discard pile, and makes and then adds to any melds he chooses before discarding. A meld is a set of matching cards, three or more of the same rank, or of the same suit in sequence. The joker is wild and can be used in a meld to represent any card. If it is at one end of a sequence (e.g. 4 and 5 of clubs plus joker) and a player has the card it replaces (in this case the 3 or 6 of clubs) he can swap them over. This can only be done once with each joker. Aces count high or low, but not both, so king-ace-two is not a meld.

The winner is the player who gets rid of all his cards in melds. If stock runs out before anyone has won, the discard pile is turned over to form a new stock. This only applies the first time stock is exhausted. If it happens again, both players put the appropriate money into a pool which goes to the winner of the next hand. Timing is all in Coon Can – try to keep melds in the hand for as long as possible without being stuck with them if your opponent looks as if he may be near ending the game.

The loser pays one unit for every pip on the cards left in his hand, with jokers counting 15, aces 11, and court cards 10.

Variation

★ **COLONEL** Only one pack is used, with no jokers. Play is as for Coon Can, but at any stage either player can 'challenge' the other. If the challenge is accepted, both hands are shown and counted, and whoever has the lowest count is the winner and receives the difference between his and his opponent's score. Aces and court cards count 10, others by face value.

To win at this game, melds should be made earlier, and you should try to save only low cards in your hand. If you feel your opponent may be about to go out, challenge him.

ECARTE

★ **OBJECTIVE:**   to build a trick-winning hand.

Take a standard deck and remove all cards from two to six inclusive, leaving you with 32 cards. These rank king, queen, jack, ace, 10, 9, 8, 7. Five cards are dealt in twos and ones, and the next is turned up to denote trumps. If it is a king, dealer scores one point immediately. The rest of the pack forms the stock.

Non-dealer examines his hand and decides if he wants to play it. He says either 'I play', in which case play starts straight away, or 'I propose' if he does not like his hand. If he proposes, dealer can say either 'I play', in which case play starts anyway, or 'I accept', which is a signal that both can change any number of cards in their hand. Starting with the non-dealer, they discard face down onto a pile and draw the same number of cards from stock.

After this, the process is repeated until play begins. If the stock runs out, players are stuck with the cards in their hands.

If either holds the king of trumps, he can announce it before he plays the first trick (which is started by the non-dealer), and scores a point. This is not compulsory. Whoever leads for each trick states its suit, and his opponent must follow this if he is able to, otherwise trump or discard.

Winning all five tricks is called a 'vole'. If the hands are played as originally dealt, whoever called 'I play' scores a point if he makes the most tricks and two for a vole. If he makes fewer tricks than his opponent, his opponent scores two points. However, if cards were changed at the beginning, scoring is 1 point per round and 2 for vole. The target is 5 points.

Obviously much hinges on the players' decisions on when to play. Basically if you are dealt a hand with plenty of trumps or at least one trump and high cards in other suits, it is worth the gamble of playing before your opponent exchanges his hand for a better one. Equally, if your opponent discards only one or two cards (indicating a strong base) you should cut your losses and opt to play.

EIGHTS (SNOOKER or SWEDISH RUMMY)

★ *OBJECTIVE:*   to get rid of all your cards.

Cards and suits have no rank in this game, in which players are dealt a hand of seven cards, the remainder forming the stock and the top card turned face up as the 'starter'.

Non-dealer begins by adding a card to the starter pile that matches the previous card in either rank or suit. So if the card on the pile is the six of diamonds, any six or any diamond will do. The aim is to get rid of your hand.

If he has no suitable card in his hand, or chooses not to play one, he takes cards from stock until he can play. If stock has run out, he passes. Eights are wild, and can be played at any turn, when the player can name a new suit which his opponent must then follow (unless he plays an eight).

First player to run out of cards wins, and collects from his opponent the value of his remaining cards, calculated as follows:

Eights	50
Kings, queens, jacks or tens	10
Aces	1
Other cards face value	

If the game cannot continue but both players have cards left, the lowest count wins, and collects the difference. The target is the first to 100 points.

Variations

★ *WILD JACKS* Jacks are wild instead of eights. All other rules apply.

★ *ROCKAWAY* The turned over card is known as the 'widow'. Aces take the place of eights as wild cards. Here the loser's remaining cards are counted and scored, with aces counting 15, court cards 10, and other cards their face value.

★ *HOLLYWOOD EIGHTS* Here the values are:

Eights	20
Aces	15
Face cards	10
Other cards face value	

100 points wins each stage, but the score sheet is set up for three simultaneous stages. The first hand won by each play is only scored in stage one. The second hand is scored in stages one and two. After this, wins are scored in all games. Example:

Stage 1		Stage 2		Stage 3	
A	B	A	B	A	B
30		35		40	
65		75			
105					

Here player A won the first stage by 30 points, and the second by 35. This second score is recorded both in the stage 2 column, and added to his score in game 1. Once a player has 100 or more points in game 1, he has won that stage and subsequent scores by either player are added from stage 2 onwards, until each one totals more than 100 points. Three stages are usually played, although obviously these can take up a much higher number of rounds to play. The winner is whoever wins two or more stages.

EUCHRE

★ **OBJECTIVE:**   to win tricks, judging how many you are likely to win in advance.

Two-handed Euchre is played with a pack of 33 cards: a standard deck with every value from six down removed, plus a joker. Aces rank highest except in the trump suit, which is ranked joker, jack (known as the right bower), jack of same colour (the left bower), then ace, king and so on.

The aim of the game is to win three ('point', scoring one) or five ('march', scoring two) tricks. A bidder who fails to make at least one point is 'euchred', and his opponent scores two points. The target is five points, although a higher total of 7 or ten can be agreed.

The dealer supplies hands of five in bundles of three then two cards, and the top card of the pack is turned up to propose trumps.

Non-dealer has first say on accepting the trump suit. He examines his hand and judges whether he is likely to make a point (three tricks) with that suit as trumps. If he is, he says 'I order it up', and the dealer must take up the upturned card and discard one from his hand. If the non-dealer is not so confident, he passes.

Similarly, dealer says either 'I take it up' and makes his discard, or 'I turn it down', in which case he puts the trump card underneath the pack. In the latter situation, non-dealer can now name the trump suit in which he feels he can make three tricks, and play commences. If he does not think he can make point, he passes, and the choice is down to the dealer. If he, too, is unable to name a suit, a new deal is made. Non-dealer always leads, and tricks are then played out and scored.

Remember that to name or accept a suit you must be sure of winning three tricks, which requires good trumps or the joker and one of the bower jacks.

Variation

★ Some people play two-handed Euchre with a smaller pack of 24 (all cards between eight and two inclusive removed, and no joker).

Some of the non-dealer's early advantage if he selects trumps can be reduced if players agree in advance to continue turning over cards to propose trumps until one player accepts them.

FIVE HUNDRED

★ *OBJECTIVE:*   to win a specified number of tricks.

For this game you need 33 cards: a deck with every card between six and two inclusive removed, and one joker added. Cards rank from ace (high) to seven, except in trumps, when the order is joker, jack (right bower), jack of the same colour as the trump suit (left bower), ace, king, queen and so on. For bidding purposes, suits are also ranked, from hearts (high), diamonds, clubs, spades.

Three cards each are dealt, with another hand of three to the centre, forming the 'widow'. Then another seven cards are dealt to each player (in fours, then threes), but not the widow. Players then bid on their hands, with the final bid (the contract) being made before both players pass. The bid represents how many tricks you can win with a certain suit as trumps, or with no trumps (all suits of equal rank). Minimum bid is six tricks. If neither player bids, the hand is dealt again. The bids are valued as follows:

	Six	Seven	Eight	Nine	Ten
Spades	40	140	240	340	440
Clubs	60	160	260	360	460
Diamonds	80	180	280	380	480
Hearts	100	200	300	400	500
No-trumps	120	220	320	420	520

Highest bidder picks up the widow and discards three cards from his hand, face down, before leading for the first trick. Tricks are won by the highest card of the suit led, or the highest trump if a player has none of that suit remaining. In no-trumps, the joker beats any card, but can only be used if the player has a void in the suit led. If it is led, that player states which suit it represents. Each player keeps his won tricks separate so that the game can be scored.

If the bidder makes his contract he scores as in the table above. If the bid was worth under 250 points and that player takes all 10 tricks, he scores 250. If he fails to achieve his bid, its value is deducted from his score. (A minus score is known as being in the 'hole'). His opponent scores 10 points for every trick won, whether or not the contract is made. The target is 500 points. If both players achieve this, the bidder wins.

Bidding is a matter of experience but obviously four cards of the same suit should encourage you to bid it as trumps, and aces are guaranteed trick winners unless trumped or 'jokered'. In play, it pays to get your trumps out early, leading from the top of the suit down, then play your longest suit.

Variation

★ *NULLO* Nullo is an extra bid to win no tricks in no-trumps, and is worth 250 points. If he fails (by winning at least one trick) he loses 250 points and his opponent scores 10 points for each trick the nullo bidder won.

FROGS IN THE POND

★ *OBJECTIVE:*   to capture key cards by playing tricks.

The dealer deals ten cards each, two at a time. He then deals ten cards face down in the centre of the table – these are the 'frogs in the pond'. The aim is to score 100 points by winning certain cards. Points values are:

Tens	10
Fives	5
Aces	4
Kings	3
Queens	2
Jacks	1

The non-dealer leads a card, and his opponent must follow suit if he can, on penalty of 10 points. The winner of each trick takes the cards plus one of the 'frogs', which he examines and places face down on the won trick, before leading for the next. There are no trumps.

When all cards have been played, scores are totalled, including the added frogs, the deck reshuffled and play begins again, the target being 100 points.

WHIST (see German Whist page 33)

There are a number of versions of Whist, but most rely on having four players in partnerships. German Whist is the best variant for two players.

GERMAN WHIST

★ *OBJECTIVE:*   to build a winning hand of 13.

Two hands of 13 are dealt, and the next card is turned over to denote trumps. Tricks are played out in the usual way, but the winner of the first trick takes the face-up card, waits for his opponent to draw from stock, then turns over the next card. When all cards have been drawn, the hands are played out in the usual way, the lead going to whoever won the last trick of the first stage of the game. Thus, the aim of the first phase is to build-up a strong hand, and keep an eye on what cards are played (and therefore dead) and what your opponent picks up. The winner scores the difference in the number of tricks won (one point per trick), and the target score is 50, although it can be set lower.

OTHER FORMS OF WHIST

★ *DOUBLE DUMMY WHIST* Four hands are dealt, and after the opening lead, two dummy hands (one opposite each player) are exposed, each to be played by one player in partnership with his own hand. Lower in the cut deals and the dealer may choose which side of his opponent he sits. The seat to the right is better as it permits leading through the concealed hand. The winner of each round scores the number of tricks over six won (so eight tricks scores two). Game is the first to five points, and there are three games in a rubber.

★ *HUMBUG WHIST* A variant of Double Dummy, in which the two players sit opposite each other. Four 13-cards are dealt, the last card being turned over to denote trumps. Both players examine their hands and have the option of exchanging them for the hands to their right, facing down the original hand. Trumps stay the same even if the trump card shown is exchanged. The face-down cards are not used in play. Scoring is as for Double Dummy Whist.

★ *TRUMP HUMBUG WHIST* In this variant the trump is decided by the dealer after examining his hand, which he cannot exchange, while his opponent still has the chance to exchange his hand for the one to his right.

★ *SCOTCH WHIST (also known as CATCH THE TEN)* All cards below six are removed, leaving a deck of 36. Ranking is as usual, except the jack of trumps beats all. Six hands of six are dealt, so that each player has three hands. These hands are played independently in turns, alternating with that of the other player. Certain cards have scoring values when won in tricks:

Jack of trumps	11
Ten	10
Ace	4
King	3
Queen	2

First player to 41 wins. Note that although the ten scores high, it can still be defeated by the cards ranked above it. Since it has such a high value, capturing it is extremely useful – hence the alternative name for the game.

HEARTS

★ *OBJECTIVE:* to avoid winning tricks involving hearts cards.

The game of Hearts is based not on winning tricks but on avoiding winning tricks in which a heart is played, as each heart taken in a trick counts as a penalty point. Two hands of 13 cards are dealt, the remainder forming the stock. Non-dealer leads for the first trick, which is played out in usual way, with players obliged to follow suit if they can. There are no trumps.

Before leading for the next trick, the winner draws

the top card from stock, and his opponent the next. This continues until the stock has run out when the hands are then played out to the end. The player with fewer hearts in his won tricks at the end is the winner by the difference between the totals, each heart scoring 1, and lowest score winning. Five hands, or playing until one player has scored 30 points, is a reasonable limit.

JULEPE

★ *OBJECTIVE:*   to build a trick-winning hand.

This gambling game is played with a standard deck plus one joker, which is worth 10.5 and is wild in play – but if turned up to denote trumps, it is treated as a spade. Each player puts a token in a central pot, forming the winnings to be played for in the five tricks to be played.

Hands of nine cards are dealt in groups of three, and the next card turned up denotes trumps. The non-dealer has two options: to play the first card; or pass, indicating that he does not want to play the hand. If non-dealer passes, dealer can choose whether to insist that the hand is played, or pass, in which case the pack is shuffled and redealt.

Once a player has opted to play, both players must reduce their hands to five cards to play the game. First, they have the option of drawing up to five cards to improve their hand. The non-dealer has first chance to say how many he is discarding and how many he wishes to draw. After this process he must be left with five cards. So if he discards six cards, he can draw two, leaving a hand of five. The dealer repeats the process.

Whoever said 'play' first now leads, and the five tricks are played. The winner must have won at least three tricks, and he gets the contents of the pot.

LOO

★ **OBJECTIVE:**   to build a trick-winning hand.

A 32-card pack, ace, king, queen, jack, ten, nine, eight and seven, is prepared for this gambling game, with aces high and sevens low, and the dealer must put a stake of three tokens into the pool before play commences. He then deals three hands of three cards, (one each plus one in an extra hand called 'miss'), then turns up the next card to denote trumps.

The non-dealer has choices: playing with the cards dealt him; exchanging his cards for the 'miss' hand (gambling that it might be better – after all, he has nothing to lose as his tokens are not at stake); or not playing at all, in which case he discards his hand and the pack is shuffled for another deal. If he decides to play, the dealer has the same choices. If the dealer opts not to play, he takes out two tokens (leaving one as a penalty and bonus for the next game) and the deal goes to his opponent.

Non-dealer leads for the first trick, and throughout the game players must follow suit if possible, or trump. If a player holds the ace of trumps, or the king if the ace was turned over, he must lead it. If a player holds more than one trump, he must lead the higher one first. Winning a trick earns a token from the pool, but if a player wins none, he is 'looed' and must put in three tokens, forming the pool for the next hand.

Variations

★ **FIVE CARD LOO** As you may gather, each player receives five cards, and thus the pool must be five tokens. No miss hand is dealt, but once they have agreed to play that round, players may exchange any number of cards by discarding and drawing from stock.

The jack of clubs is a wild card, the highest trump

in the pack (known as 'pam'), but cannot be played in a trick if the opponent lays down the ace of trumps and says 'Pam be civil'. If a player has five cards of a suit, or four plus pam, he shows it and automatically wins the hand.

★ *IRISH LOO* Each player is dealt three cards, but there is no miss or pam, and cards can be exchanged from stock. If the upturned card denoting trumps is a club, neither player has the option to pass the hand, which must be played out.

NAPOLEON

★ *OBJECTIVE:*   to make the number of tricks bid for.

Five cards each are dealt for this gambling game, and each player has one chance to bid (make a contract to win a certain number of tricks) or pass. The lowest bid allowed is two. A bid of 'five' is called Napoleon, or Nap. The highest bidder starts, his first card played denoting the trump suit. Tricks are then played out in the usual way. If successful, the bidder receives one token for each trick of his contract, unless it was Napoleon, for which he is paid 10. If he did not make his contract, he pays one token for each shortfall, five for Nap.

Variations

★ *WELLINGTON* This variant allows an additional bid to beat Napoleon, also for five tricks, but at double the stakes, and called a Wellington. If the Napoleon bidder still thinks he can make five tricks, he calls 'Blucher', a contract at triple stakes.

★ *MISERY* A further bid that can be allowed is misère, or misery, which is a contract to lose all five tricks, without a trump suit, and for exactly the same stake as Napoleon.

OKLAHOMA

★ **OBJECTIVE:**   to make high scoring melds.

The joker features in this superb game as the additional card to two decks, making 105 cards.

Hands of 13 are dealt and the top card of stock turned over. The aim of the game is to form melds (sequences of three or more cards of the same suit, or sets of three or more cards of the same rank), which are laid down as they are made. The joker and all twos act as wild cards (as in Canasta, see page 61), and are used to supplement the melds. Aces count high or low but cannot be used to go 'round the corner', linking king and two.

The non-dealer has the option of picking up the turned-up card, which must be immediately melded, and another card from the hand discarded. If he does not take it, the dealer has the same choice. Play continues with each player drawing either from stock or the discard pile, making any melds he can, and discarding. Cards taken from the discard pile must be melded immediately, and the rest of the pile is picked up and joins the player's hand.

A melded sequence can number up to 14 cards (a complete suit with an ace at each end), but a set of equal rank cards cannot number more than four. If a wild card is used, the card it represents must be announced, to prevent it being falsely used later on. In the case of the joker, if the card it represents comes into the player's hand, or appears on the discard pile, they can be exchanged and the joker re-enters play.

The queen of spades can only be discarded if it is the player's last card, and the game ends when a player runs out of cards, or when the stock runs out. Players must discard as their final move when going out, thus a player with less than three cards can only go out by adding to his existing melds, even if he draws one from stock that completes a sequence in his hand – because he still has to discard to go out.

At the end of the game, melds are scored as follows:

Card	Melded	In hand
Joker	100	−200
Queen of spades	50	−100
Aces	20	−20
Kings to eights	10	−20
Sevens to threes	5	−5

Twos count minus 20 in the hand, but in melds score as for the card they represent.

Going out earns a bonus of 100 points, but going out anytime after the second turn with a completely hidden hand (i.e. no melds on show) scores 250. The winning total is 1,000 points.

RACING DEMON

★ **OBJECTIVE:**   to get rid of your demon pile.

This fiendish game is a variation of the popular Demon version of solitaire, and begins with both players holding one pack of cards each, with different colour backs. Both deal 13 cards face down into a pile, and these are known as the demons. The top cards are faced up, and each player deals four cards face up from the stock, laying them to the right of the demon pile. These cards can be built on in descending order of opposite colours, i.e. black, red, black, red and so on, using cards either from the stock or from the demon as they turn up.

As aces become available, they are placed separately face up, eventually forming eight piles which either player can build upon. These are built up in ascending order in suit, from ace to king. Cards can be transferred from other piles to these stacks but cannot be removed.

Each player is aiming to get rid of his demon pile – the 13 cards originally dealt. The stock is turned up in sets of three. If the player can position the top card he does so, making the next card in stock available, and so on. Cards which cannot be played from stock go into a discard pile, which becomes stock when the original stock is exhausted.

The three of clubs in stock can be put on the opponent's foundation pile. Then there is a race for each to place the four of clubs!

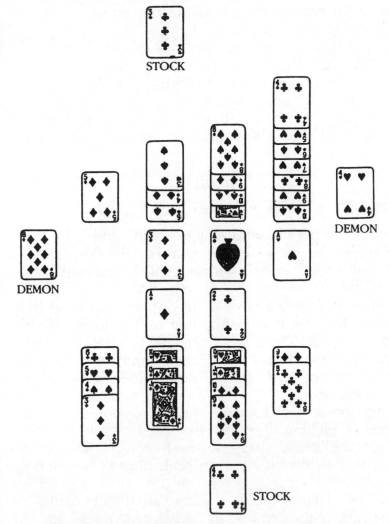

The eight of diamonds in demon can go onto the third column.

The winner is the first to get rid of his demon. This game is played at a furious pace with countless frustrations as your opponent manages to place a card on a pile you were about to add to yours.

Scoring

The winner scores 10 points and both players score 1 point for each of their cards in the centre. The player with cards left in demon doubles the number and subtracts this from the number of cards in the centre to establish his final score (you will discover to your horror that minus scores are quite possible!). Should you reach the point where kings are piled on the foundations, an extra 10 points is given to whoever placed each king. The winner is the first to reach 200 points.

RUMMY

★ *OBJECTIVE:*   to build melds in the hand.

Rummy is a popular and easy to learn game with many variations. The most basic version is described first, but you may prefer to start with one of the variants – they are all fun.

Dealer deals eight cards to his opponent, and seven to himself. The aim is to be the first to 'lay down' all your cards in melds. These are groups of at least three cards in runs (sequences) of consecutive numbers of the same suit, or sets of cards of the same value. In sequences, aces count low.

The non-dealer discards, and his opponent has the choice of picking up either that card or one from the top of the stock, decides whether it is useful, and discards. Play continues, with both players building up their melds in secret. When one can get rid of all his cards by laying melds (using all eight cards, or discarding one to empty his hand) he does so and the game is over. If this had not happened when the stock runs out, the discard pile is turned over as stock and the game goes on.

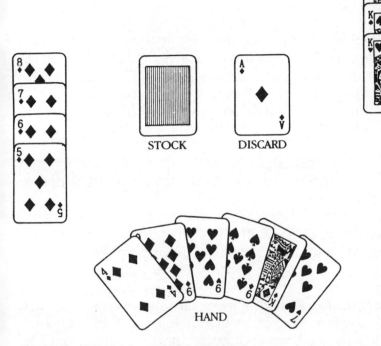

STOCK   DISCARD

HAND

Player can add 4 to meld, place the three nines as a meld, the King on his opponent's meld, and discard the 7 to go out.

Variations

★ *RUMMY (version two)* Ten cards each are dealt, and the top card of stock is turned over to start the discard pile. The object is to create melds as described above, but these are not stored in the hand but placed face up in front of each player. Melds can only be made during a player's turn, and he can add cards to either his or his opponent's melds – because the aim is to get rid of all his cards. Any number of melds can be made or added to during one turn. A player can get rid of his last card by placing it on a meld or discarding it (although in some variations a player can only go out with a discard). When a player has gone out, he scores the value of the cards left in his opponent's hand (aces count one, court cards ten). The target is 100 points.

The end cards (king and ace) are the least likely to be melded as they would have to be at the end of a sequence so it is best to discard them first. Keep an eye on your opponent's discards – they will provide clues to what he is storing in his hand, and you will also know what cards you are more likely to be able to collect.

★ *DOUBLE RUMMY* A player who melds all his cards and goes out in one turn without having melded before scores double.

★ *ROUND THE CORNER RUMMY* This allows using the ace to meld 'round the corner' – linking the king and the two.

★ *CONTINENTAL RUMMY* This variant uses two packs, each with a joker. Players are dealt hands of 15. The only melds allowed are sequences, and these can only be made at the end of the game to go out. Jokers are wild cards and replace any other card. The winner collects a point for winning, and two for each joker left in his opponent's hand. The target is 11 points. If you wish, this variation can be played without adding the jokers.

★ *GIN RUMMY* Ten cards each are dealt, and the top cards of stock turned over to start the discard pile. The non-dealer only has the option of taking that card: if he does not like it, he does not draw from stock, and his turn passes to the dealer. If the non-dealer passes too, the first player can now take a card from stock.

Once again the aim is to make melds, but any unmatched cards in your hand count against you. If this score is 10 points or less, you have the option to go out anyway. If you go out with no unmatched cards at all, you call 'Gin', and score a bonus of 25 plus your opponent's unmatched cards. If you do have unmatched cards, the opponent has the chance to lay off any of his unmatched cards onto your melds before the game is officially over.

Your score of unmatched cards when you go out is deducted from that of your opponent's remaining cards. If he has less points than you, ('undercuts') he scores a 25 bonus.

However, if neither player had gone out before the last two cards are drawn, the deal is abandoned without scoring. The target is 100 points.

RUSSIAN BANK

★ **OBJECTIVE:**   to get rid of all your cards.

Players use one pack each, with a different coloured back to that of their opponent. Each lays out four cards, face up, slightly to their right, in line towards the other player. The eight cards make up the tableau, and there should be sufficient space in the middle for a further two rows. Each then places the next 13 cards in his deck face down. This is his stock, and its top card is turned up.

The remaining cards are placed face down in front of each player. Any aces which have appeared so far are now put in line next to the player's line of four cards in the tableau. These piles are called foundations.

Whoever had the lower value first tableau card starts the game by beginning to place cards in sequence on one of the eight foundations. Cards must be played to foundations when they become available, and cannot then be moved. If no cards can be played to the foundation, a player may make placements in descending sequence, alternating in colour, onto the rest of the tableau. Cards must be added in such a way that all cards in the sequence are visible. Only the top card is available for play, but available cards can be transferred to other piles. When it is his turn, a player can use a card from his opponent's stock.

The top card from stock is always available for play, and if it can go on a foundation pile, it must be put there. It can also be played on the tableau, or put onto an available card in the opponent's stock in a sequence going either way, as long as it is in the same suit. A player can also 'feed' cards to his opponent from the tableau or from his own hand, but cannot feed cards to his own stock. If a player does not want to make a play, he turns up the top card of his hand, and places it face up on one side of the discard pile.

Once a player has discarded, it is his opponent's turn again. Once his hand is exhausted, he turns over the discard pile and this becomes his hand. If a player does not use the last card of his hand, it cannot be used on his next turn – he starts from the discard pile.

When a space appears in the tableau, it must be filled by a card from stock or an available card in the tableau. If none are available from stock, a space can be filled from the discard pile or the hand.

The game ends when a player has no cards left in his hand, stock and discard pile. He scores 1 point for each card left in his opponent's hand or discard pile, and two for every card left in stock. He also gets a 30-point win bonus. If neither player gets rid of all his cards, the game is drawn.

Variation
★ *SINGLE DECK RUSSIAN BANK* In this variation, the aim is to build on the tableau piles or the opponent's stock.

Each player receives 26 cards in twos and then threes. The non-dealer lays his first four cards out in a row, to form the first part of the tableau. Cards available for builds are played on each other in sequence and in the same suit.

Cards can be built in either ascending or descending sequence, and this direction must be maintained. The

RUSSIAN BANK – Typical layout. All cards in tableau must be visible.

Player A can play the 10 from his hand onto the red six on the opposite tableau.

47

sequence can go round the corner' – i.e. from ace to king or vice versa. Spaces in the tableau are filled by cards the non-dealer turns from his hand one at a time, and the non-dealer can make any other builds thus created. When he turns a card that cannot be used in play, he leaves it face up on the discard pile.

The dealer then turns up four cards to complete the tableau, and plays using all eight piles until he has to discard, when it is his opponent's turn again. Cards from the tableau cannot be used to build on an opponent's pile, and it is permitted to move an entire pile from one part of the tableau to continue a sequence in the same suit and direction in another pile. Spaces in the tableau must otherwise be filled by cards from the hand or discard pile. When the top card of the discard pile is played, the one under it becomes available.

When a player's hand is exhausted, he turns over his discard pile and deals a new hand. The game ends when either player runs out of cards or playing opportunities. Scoring is as in Russian Bank, except there is no score for cards left in stock.

SEVEN-UP

★ **OBJECTIVE:**   to build a trick winning hand.

The name of this game is derived from the fact that it takes seven points to win. Hands of six cards each are dealt three at a time, and the next card is turned up and placed on top of the stock. If it is a jack, dealer scores one point.

The non-dealer examines his hand and decides if the upturned card is a satisfactory trump suit. If he is happy, he 'stands', and trumps are set (if the upturned card is a jack, dealer now scores one point). If he is not, he 'begs', passing the decision to the dealer, who must either give his opponent a point to let the trump stand, or deal three new cards each and turn over another card. If the suit is the same, the process is repeated, until a new trump is agreed. The last card cannot be turned for trumps, and if the pack is exhausted the players (probably equally exhausted) start the whole game again.

Once trumps is set, each player discards as many cards as necessary, face down, to be left with a hand of six. Tricks are now played for and one point is won for each of the following:

High: The player dealt the highest trump in play.

Low: The player dealt the lowest trump in play.

Jack: Whoever wins the jack of trumps in a trick (unless the dealer turned it over for the trump decider).

Game: Highest total of point values for cards taken in tricks.

Values are ace 4, king 3, queen 2, jack 1, tens 10. Other cards have no value. If only one trump is played, it scores two for both high and low (3 if it is the jack). If both counts are equal, no point is awarded for game.

First player to gather seven points wins. If both players achieve this in the same hand, points are scored in the order of events above. If the dealer has six points and turns the jack, he wins.

Variations

★ *ALL FIVES* In this variation points are also scored for winning the following trumps in a trick: ten 10, five 5, ace 4, king 3, queen 2, jack 1. First to 61 wins the game.

★ *CALIFORNIA JACK* Each player receives six cards, and the stock is placed face up, the top card denoting trumps. Winner of the first trick takes this card and his opponent the next. Play continues until all cards in the stock and hand are exhausted. Then each player goes through his trick pile and scores a point each for high (ace of trumps), low (two of trumps), jack of trumps, and for game. The target is seven or ten points and all other rules are as in Seven-Up.

★ **SHASTA SAM** This is played as California Jack but the stock is kept face down so the winner of each trick does not know what card he will draw. Trumps are decided by a single cut of the pack.

SOLOMON

★ **OBJECTIVE:** to build a good Poker hand.

The game of Solomon requires an understanding of what makes a good Poker hand. The basics are that from five cards you want to achieve one of the following hands, in descending order of value:

Royal straight flush: Ace, king, queen, jack, ten, in the same suit.

Straight flush: A sequence in the same suit. If two players have straight flushes, the highest top card wins.

Fours: Four of the same value. Again, highest card wins a tie.

Full house: Three of the same value, and two of another. Highest three and then two wins.

Flush: Any five cards of the same suit, not in sequence.

Straight: Five cards in sequence regardless of suits. Ace ranks high or low.

Threes: Three cards of the same value.

Two pairs: Two pairs of the same value.

One pair: One pair of the same value.

Ten cards are dealt face up on the table, then the dealer hands the pack to his opponent. He now deals himself six cards, and, keeping them concealed, assesses their value if some could be exchanged with the cards on the table to produce a good poker hand. He then divides the cards on the table into two hands of five, and places the six cards face down in the centre. The dealer has the choice of which hand to take, and once he has chosen, he can change as many as he likes by discarding from his hand and drawing from the pack of six. When he has done this, the non-dealer can also draw from the pack, and then both hands are shown.

Solomon is a game of strategy and bluff, in which the non-dealer guesses which hand his opponent will choose, and arranges the six blind cards accordingly. When you get the hand of it, it is great fun!

SPINADO

★ **OBJECTIVE:**   to get rid of all your cards.

For this gambling game, remove all twos plus the eight of diamonds from the pack, and draw for dealer. He must put 12 tokens into a central pot, and the non-dealer puts in three. Three hands are then dealt, of 15 cards for each player and 17 to a third hand, which is called the 'widow'.

Non-dealer starts by playing a card, announcing its rank and value. Whoever has the next card up in sequence then plays that card, and so play continues until the king (or in diamonds, the seven) is reached. Whoever plays the last card starts the next sequence. All aces are stops. The player who gets rid of all his cards first wins the pot, and receives another token for every card left in his opponent's hand.

Stakes are won during the game for playing certain cards. The ace of diamonds is Spinado, and scores 3 tokens, and is played as a second card in a turn to stop the sequence. So, if you are in clubs and play the eight, nine and ten but do not have the jack, you can play the ace, and start the next sequence.

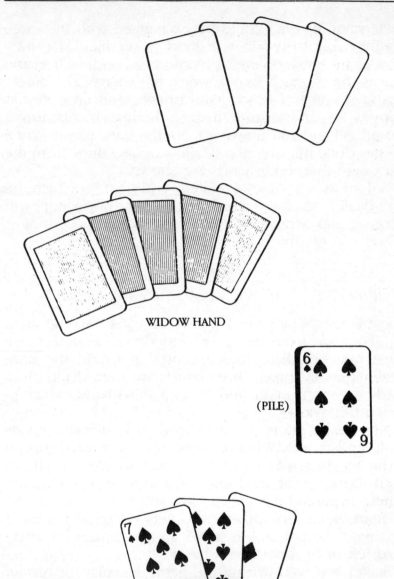

WIDOW HAND

(PILE)

This player is about to win by playing the 7 and 8 of spades and the stripper Ace of Diamonds. He receives four tokens for the four cards in his opponent's hand.

The diamond court cards have scoring values too. The king is worth two tokens, and if the same player puts down the queen he scores 12, and the queen and jack are worth another six, provided both are played by the same player. If the loser has Spinado in his hand at the end, he pays double for each card in his hand. However, in tactical terms, it is worth holding on to Spinado for as long as your dare, as it can act as a stopper in a suit you have no more cards in.

TABLANETTE

★ **OBJECTIVE:** to pick up most cards from the table.

In this game the value of cards is king 14, queen 13, jack 12, ace 1 or 11, other cards face value. Six cards each are dealt, and four left face up on the table. If the non-dealer then plays a card of the same value as any of the exposed four, he picks it up. If the value of any two or three cards on the table equals that of his card, he takes them. He may be able to do both these things: if the four exposed cards are the queen, ten, seven and three, and he plays a queen, he picks up the queen, plus the ten and the three (because they add up to 13). Cards taken in this way are piled to one side of each player.

If a player is able to take all exposed cards with one play (sometimes there is only one left), he calls 'tablanette' and scores the total face value of all the cards, including the one he plays.

Play continues until each has played his six cards. If someone makes tablanette, the opponent must play a card onto the table. This should either be a card of the lowest posssible value (to give his opponent a minimum score) or one he thinks his opponent will not be able to match (he may know this by having watched the cards played before).

When each player has played his six cards, a further six each are dealt, and the game continues. When the last six have been played, any cards left on the table are taken by the last player to take a card from it. Each then scores from his pile one point for every card from ace to ten, and one for the two of clubs, two for the ten of diamonds. The player with more cards scores a bonus of three. The pack is shuffled and play continues until someone scores 251 or more points.

YUKON

★ *OBJECTIVE:*   to win tricks and capture certain cards.

In this game jacks are called 'yukons' and are the highest value cards, taking the place of trumps. The jack of spades is the 'grand yukon' and ranks above the others. Each player receives five cards, and the non-dealer leads for the first trick.

Players must follow suit or, if they cannot, play a yukon or discard. Highest card wins, with yukons ranked above the ace. If two yukons are played, the first wins, unless the second is the grand yukon. After each trick the winner places the two cards involved face down in front of them, and takes the top card from stock, after which his opponent takes the next. Hands are played out until stock is exhausted. Players then score for cards won in tricks as follows:

Grand yukon   15
Other yukons   10
Tens   10
Aces   5
Kings   3
Queens   2

The target is 250 points or more. If scores are equal, whoever took the ace of spades wins.

LEVEL THREE

BEZIQUE

★ **OBJECTIVE:** to score points through winning key tricks and making melds.

Bezique is played with a 64-card deck, comprising two standard decks with the cards valued two to six removed. So the rank of cards is ace high to seven low.

Players agree a winning total score, usually 1,000, 1,500 or 2,000 points, arrived at by adding points scored in melds and tricks won by each player.

Melds and their values:

Meld	Points
Trump marriage (king and queen of trumps)	40
No-trump marriage	20
Ace, ten, king, queen, jack of trumps	250
Queen of spades and jack of diamonds (bezique)	40
Pairs of the above sequence (double bezique)	500
Any four aces	100
Any four kings	80
Any four queens	60
Any four jacks	40

Melds must be scored immediately as the cards can be replayed.

Each ace or ten (called a brisque) taken in a trick counts 10 points. The dealer receives 10 points if he turns a seven as trump card, and on winning a trick either player may exchange a seven of trumps for the trump face up on the table. Or he can show the seven and score 10. Ten points are also given for winning the last trick.

Each player is dealt eight cards, first three at a time, then a pair, then the final trio. The next card is turned face up and denotes trumps. The deal alternates between players.

The non-dealer plays a card, and his opponent responds with the trick won by the highest of the suit led or the (highest) trump. If identical cards are played, the first wins the trick. The winner keeps the trick cards face down, and can then make a maximum of one meld, before drawing the first card from the top of the stock, followed by his opponent.

The holder may lead or play a card in a meld as if it were in his hand. A card may be used in different melds, but not twice in the same one. For example, a queen of spades may be used to score in four melds: a marriage, sequence, bezique, and four queens. But once four queens have been melded, and one of the queens played, another queen may not be added to create a 'new' meld. So if the bezique is melded as 40 points, a second bezique can be added to make a double bezique, scoring an additional 500 points. A double bezique melded in one turn scores only 500 points.

Melding ceases as soon as one face down card and the trump card remain in the stock. The winner of the next trick takes the hidden card, his opponent the trump, and each picks up all his melds. Then the last eight tricks are played, with players required to follow suit and to win tricks if they can.

Brisques are scored at once and not at the end of the hand. The game is over when the first player reaches the agreed total of points.

The strategy of Bezique is that players should strive to

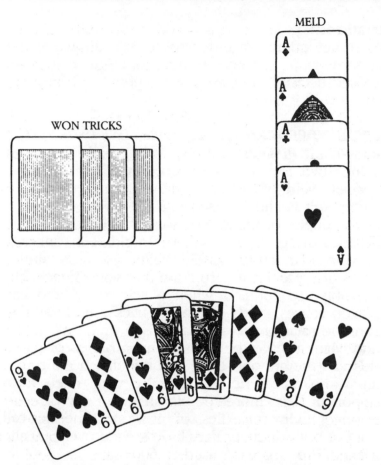

Having won the trick, the player made his meld and picked up the Queen of Spades to go with his Jack of Diamonds, making a Bezique. He wins the next trick with an ace from his meld, and places his Bezique meld.

save cards that may be turned into declarations of melds. So queens and jacks are by far the most important, and queens of spades and jacks of diamonds should always be saved. If four of a kind is scored, always play one of them so that the same meld can be scored again. Leads should be designed to force the opponent to give up cards which might form melds in the future if retained.

Variations

★ First melded marriage decides trumps. No-trump card is turned up. Instead, the first marriage melded and scored decides the trump suit. There is no score for the seven of trumps.

★ *FIVE HUNDRED BEZIQUE (also called ONE-DECK BEZIQUE or FRENCH PINOCHLE)* A 32-card deck is used, with values two to six inclusive removed. An additional special meld of ace-king-queen-jack-ten of any no-trump suit is allowed, scoring 120 points.

The queen of spades and jack of diamonds meld is called 'binage'. Once a card is melded it cannot be used to form another meld. Values of cards taken in tricks are: ace 11, ten 10, king 4, queen 3, jack 2.

Points are counted when play is over, and each player scores cards taken in tricks, and keeps a running total of melds. Game is over at 500 points, and when a player believes he has reached or passed this total he announces it, and this can be during or after a hand. If he is right, he wins even if his opponent has more points. If he is wrong, the opponent wins regardless of his score. If neither calls out but both discover they have scored over 500 after a hand, the target is raised to 600.

★ *POLISH BEZIQUE* The winner of a trick removes any picture cards it contains, together with the ten of trumps if played, and keeps them, face up, separate from his melds. They may then be added to melds as he sees fit, but cannot be used in play.

★ *RUBICON BEZIQUE* This is played with a deck of 128 cards, formed from four 52-card decks with all values between two and six inclusive removed. Two nine-card hands are dealt, one alternate card at a time, with the rest placed face down.

The non-dealer takes one card from stock, plays the first card, and the dealer can only win the trick with a higher card of the same suit. Trumps are not decided until the first marriage or sequence is melded, when its suit becomes trumps for the hand. Trumps come into play after this. If the same card is played by both players, the one led wins. The winner of each trick draws the top card from stock, and his opponent takes the next. Cards won in tricks prior to the introduction of trumps have no scoring value.

In addition to the standard melds of Bezique (see page 55), the following melds are allowed in Rubicon Bezique:

A backdoor: Ace, king, queen, jack and ten of trumps. 150 points.
Triple Bezique: Three queens of spades and three jacks of diamonds, laid down as a single meld. 1,500 points.
Quadruple Bezique: Four queens of spades and four jacks of diamonds, laid in a single meld. 4,500 points.
Carte Blanche: An originally dealt hand with no picture cards. 50 points. This must be shown to the opponent. Every subsequent time the player fails to draw a picture card he scores another 50 points.

Scoring is very different from standard two-handed Bezique. A player may break up a meld by playing one or more cards from it, then add cards to it and score the whole meld again. Players do not gather tricks they have won which do not have point-valued cards (aces or tens), until a brisque is played. Then, the winner of that trick takes in all previously played cards. If he fails to do this, and his opponent wins the next trick containing brisques, the opponent takes all the cards.

Each game comprises one deal. The higher scorer wins, and scores the difference between the two scores, plus a bonus of 500 points. Any fractions of 100 points are ignored, unless they determine the winner. Brisques are only counted if a player feels it will prevent him being rubiconed. The only score counted from the play is 50 points for the last trick. If the loser scores less than 1,000 points, he is rubiconed, and scores nothing, while the victor gets an additional 500 bonus, plus the loser's points, plus 320 points for all brisques.

★ *CHINESE BEZIQUE* This is played as Rubicon Bezique, except that a 192-card deck is used, comprising six 52-card decks from which every value between two and six inclusive have been removed. The dealer deals 12 cards each, one at a time, and in addition to the melds allowed in Rubicon Bezique, the following are used:

Meld	Points
Four aces of trumps	1,000
Four tens of trumps	900
Four kings of trumps	800
Four queens of trumps	600
Four jacks of trumps	400
Carte blanche/Winning last trick	250

Brisques are not scored, and all played cards are placed upwards in the centre of the table, where they may be freely examined. Players may also count the cards left in stock. Each played hand constitutes a game, and a game bonus of 1,000 points is made to the winner of the hand. If the loser scores under 3,000 points, he is rubiconed and his score is added to the winner's. Fractions of 100 points are ignored unless they may be decisive.

★ *SIX DECK BEZIQUE* After the 192-card pack has been shuffled, the dealer removes a portion. If this contains exactly 24 cards, he scores 250 points. However, before the cards are dealt, the non-dealer guesses the number of cards cut off the top of the deck, and if he is correct he scores 150 points. The remainder of the cards are turned face down on the table and form the stock.

★ *EIGHT DECK BEZIQUE* A 256-card is used, made from eight 52-card decks with values from two to six inclusive removed. The game is played as six deck Bezique, with each player starting with 15 cards. Scoring is as follows:

Single bezique	50
Double bezique	500
Triple bezique	1,500
Quadruple bezique	4,500
Quintuple bezique	9,000
Five aces of trumps	2,000
Five tens of trumps	1,800
Five kings of trumps	1,600
Five queens of trumps	1,200
Five jacks of trumps	800

The loser is rubiconed if he scores under 5,000 points.

CANASTA

★ *OBJECTIVE:*   to get rid of all cards into melds.

For Canasta you need two decks of cards each with two jokers – 108 cards in all. These jokers, and the eight twos in play, are wild cards, and can be substituted for any other.

You get rid of all cards from your hand by making melds – three or more cards of the same rank. A canasta is a meld of seven or more cards, and can be formed either entirely with cards of the same rank (a 'pure' canasta) or with supplementary wild cards. These can never outnumber or equal the other cards in the canasta unless it is already complete – so if you have used the limit of three wild cards to make a canasta, you are then allowed to add another wild card.

Cards have fixed scoring values:

Joker	50
Ace or two	20
King to eight	10
Seven to four	5
Threes	Different value system see below.

So a mixed canasta of five nines, a joker and a two would be worth 5 × 10 (50) plus 50 for the joker, plus 20 for the two = 120. Cards can only score once they are placed in melds face up on the table. Any cards held in the hand at the end of the game are scored against that player. Canasta is a marvellously tense game because there are often advantages in holding melds or even canastas in your hand – but if your opponent goes out first, they could score you a minus.

Canasta features a number of bonus scores, too. Going out scores 100. Going out by laying a canasta in your final turn (a concealed canasta) scores 200. Mixed canastas are worth 300, while pure canastas score 500.

The winner is the first to score 5,000.

Both players are dealt 15 cards, the remainder forming the stock which is left turned down except for the top card which is turned over and commences the discard pile (the 'pack'). If it is a wild card or a red or black three, another card is placed above it. The non-dealer draws a card from stock, makes any melds he chooses to, and discards.

From now on, players have to pick up either from stock or, if they are able and choose to, from the discard pile. To pick from the discard pile, the player must first display a meld, which must contain at least two pure cards. He can then add the top card from the discard pile to the meld, and must transfer the rest of the pile to his hand and discard to finish his turn.

As the game continues through a number of hands some conditions are placed on the first meld. If a player has a score from minus anything to 1,500, the first meld(s) must score 50 (so three aces would score 60 and be acceptable, but four fours would score only 20 and need the addition of a joker or two twos, or be supplemented by another meld worth at least 30). For scores of 1,500 to 3,000 the minimum initial meld score is 90, and above 3,000, the minimum is 120. Thus as the scores grow, it becomes harder for players to start melding. This can be a major handicap for the higher scorer, and an invaluable bonus for his opponent!

The only exception to this rule is if the discard pile card will be used to complete a canasta.

Players can make their first meld entirely from their hand without picking up from the discard pile at all, and simply draw from stock, if they choose. A player holding only one card cannot take a discard pile consisting only of one card.

Either player can 'freeze' the pack by discarding a wild card. It can only be unfrozen by a player forming a meld from his hand with two pure cards, then adding the top card from the discard pile. If the first card upturned is a wild card or a red three, the pack is also frozen.

Players can add cards to their melds during their turn, i.e. between drawing from stock or the pack, and discarding. However, cards cannot be removed from melds, so once, say, a joker is used to help form a meld, it cannot be reused to form a canasta elsewhere.

Threes are special in Canasta. Red threes are worth 100 points and are always displayed immediately they are received, with the player drawing a card from stock for each red three he has. If a player has a red three in his hand at the end of the game, he loses 500 points. If he has all four red threes on display, the bonus is increased to 800.

Typical layout of cards in Canasta – 1 pure and 1 impure Canasta, and two red threes plus melds in the making

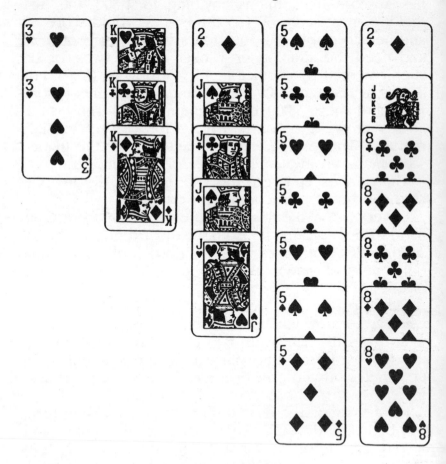

Black threes are used as 'stop' cards, freezing the pack for one turn – they cannot be picked up by a black three meld. Black threes can only be melded by a player who is going out, and cannot be mixed with wild cards.

When the stock is exhausted, the discard pile is turned over to begin it again. If stock runs out and there is only one card in the discard pile, the game ends and hands are scored, without a going out bonus.

The game ends when one player uses his last card on a meld or as a discard. He must have at least two canastas. All melds and bonuses are then scored, and the opponent's remaining hand is scored against him.

To be successful at Canasta you need nerves of steel and an eye for an opportunity. Watch what your opponent melds – you will be unable to build a pure canasta of anything he displays. Try to keep a few pairs in reserve, to use to go out by adding a wild card to form a final meld to empty your hand, or to unfreeze the pack. You may occasionally choose not to pick up the pack if it is quite thin: never turn down such an opportunity with a big pack – in the early and middle game, power often rests with the biggest hand. Obviously, you have to be careful with your discards, and if you feel your opponent has over-committed himself by displaying all his pairs in melds, you could freeze the pack, increasing your chances of picking it up.

Variations

★ Each player is dealt only 13 cards, and only one canasta is required before going out.

Another variation is to insist that no player can pick up the pack if he is not already displaying a meld.

★ *SAMBA* This version is a bit of a handful as it uses three packs, with six jokers. Hands are of 15 cards, but players drawing from stock take two cards and only discard one, so they are constantly building up their hands. In addition to sets of same value cards, same suit sequences can also be melded (though not with twos and threes), with the cards scoring as in ordinary Canasta. A Samba is a sequence of seven, which cannot be added to and is turned face down. A Samba scores 1,500, cannot include a wild card, cannot be added to from the top card of the discard pile, and counts as a canasta for going out purposes.

Wild cards cannot be added to a canasta, and the discard pile cannot be taken by adding its top card to a canasta. Indeed, a wild card cannot be used to form a meld to take the discard pile.

If one player has all six red threes he scores 1,000. Going out scores 200, and requires at least two canastas. Game is 10,000 points. The minimum count for an initial meld is as per canasta, but stays at 120 until a player has 7,000 points, after which it must be worth at least 150.

CASINO

★ **OBJECTIVE:**   to score points by capturing cards.

The dealer gives his opponent two cards face down, places a pair face up on the table, and takes two for himself. This process is repeated once, and dealing stops for the moment. After these hands have been played out, another four cards are dealt, but none added to the middle.

The object is to capture cards from the layout to score points. At each turn, each player has four options.

Pairing: matching a card from the hand with a card or cards of the same rank on the table. So if a player holds a queen, and there is a queen on the table, he pairs them face up in front of him. This is the only way court cards can be captured – by being matched, one at a time. None of the options set out below applies to court cards.

Combining: A card from the hand can capture two or more on the table if its value equals that of the target cards. For example an eight can capture an eight, two fours, a five and a three, a six and a two, or a seven and an ace (aces count low in Casino). It is not limited to taking just one combination – so one card can capture all four on the table in one turn.

Building: A player can add a card to the layout with a view to capturing the pile next turn. So if he has an eight and a two, and there is a six on the table, he places the two on the six, and announces 'building eights'. On any subsequent turn he can pick up both cards with his eights – and so can his opponent if he has an eight. More than one build can be set up by either player. So, if the same player also had an ace, and there is a seven on the table, he could build them, and pick up both builds with his eight later on.

You can also make multiple builds. If you hold two eights, and another is in the layout, you can add one to the table, announce 'building eights' and pick both up with your remaining eight. You could do this with a pair of fours, or any other multiple pile with a value of eight.

Builds can be increased in value, too. So if your opponent has an ace and a nine, he can place the ace on the eight and say 'building nines'. Ten is the maximum permissible value of builds. There is a further complication if same rank cards are used in a build. If a three is added to a three, the player can announce 'building threes' or 'building sixes'. If he is building threes, only threes can be added or used to take the pile. If he is building sixes, either player can raise the value of that particular pile.

Remember, builds can only be made from the hand, not the table, and you must have in your hand the card value of what you are building – so if you are building eights, you must be holding an eight, and must play it next turn.

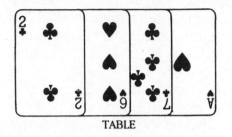

TABLE

This player can capture the whole table with his 8 – 2 and 6, and 7 and Ace

Trailing: If a player cannot pair, combine or build, or chooses not to, he must add a card face up from his hand onto the table. If his opponent has just cleared the table (made a 'sweep'), a player must trail.

Play ends when no more cards can be dealt (after the sixth hand), and any cards left on the table go to whoever made the last capture (this does not count as a sweep). Points are scored as follows:

Capturing most cards	3
Capturing most spades	1
Capturing the ten of diamonds	2
Capturing the two of spades	1
Each ace captured	1
Each sweep	1

A game can be played simply as one deal, or as first to 21 points, in which case it ends at the point the first player gains that total and the hand ceases to be played.

Variations

★ *ROYAL CASINO* This adds a further complication as the court cards have a value: jack 11, queen 12, king 13, ace 1 or 14, and can be used in building and capturing.

★ *SPADE CASINO* Spades have a higher scoring value, with each being worth one point, and ace, jack and two being worth two points. The winning target is raised to 61 points.

★ *DRAW CASINO* After the first deal and layout the remaining cards are placed face down as stock. At the end of each turn players draw one card from stock, so that they hold four cards until near the end of the game when stock has run out.

CRIBBAGE

★ *OBJECTIVE:*   to play cards to achieve a value of 31 points.

The score in Cribbage can be kept on a cribbage board, or with a pen and paper. Cards are cut and the lower card indicates dealer. Aces count low throughout the game.

Hands of six are dealt, and after examining his hand each player 'lays away' two cards, face down. The four discarded cards are set aside for later use, forming the 'crib' or 'box'. After laying off, the pack is cut and the top card of the lower half (known as the 'start') is placed face up on top of the reunited pack. If this card is a jack, the dealer scores two points.

Starting with the non-dealer, players then begin to lay

down their cards, alternately and face up in front of them, not in the centre. The aim is to be the player who places a card bringing the cumulative total to 31 points, which scores 2 game points. So if the non-dealer places a ten, and his opponent puts down a nine (calling '19'), and the non-dealer places another ten ('29'), the only cards the dealer can place are an ace or a two. If all his cards are of too high a value, he says 'go'. His opponent continues playing cards until he too cannot play without exceeding 31. Whoever plays the last card of all scores one point.

The opponent of whoever played the last card now begins a new count, starting at nought. During this stage of the game, certain combinations are also worth points. These are:

Fifteen: Laying a card to bring the count to 15 scores 2.

Pair and pair-royal: If a card of the same rank is placed, that player scores 2. If his opponent places another card of the same rank, his in turn scores 6 for a pair-royal. A fourth such card scores 12. Only matchng cards score in this way (i.e. tens and jacks are not ranked the same although they have the same value).

Run or sequence: A card which makes a sequence with the two or more just played scores 1 for each in the sequence. Suits are irrelevant, and so is the order of the cards in the sequence – so 6, 8, 7, played in that order forms a sequence. The next player can add to it with either a 5 or a 9.

All these scores must be announced and noted as they are made, and continue even if only one player is placing cards while the other passes. No combination can run from one count of 31 to another, and a run cannot contain two cards of the same rank. After this stage, each player collects his cards up again and scores further for the 'show'.

The non-dealer scores his hand plus the 'start' card, making five in all, for the following combinations:

Combinations of cards totalling 15 score 2.
Pairs score 2.
Sequences of three or more score a point for each card.
Four cards of the same suit make 'flush', and score four. If the 'start' card is in the same suit it scores another point.
Holding the jack of the same suit as the 'start' card scores one ('one for his nob').

The same card can, of course, be used in any of these combinations.

The dealer then scores his hand in the same way (using the same 'start' card), and then scores again with the four cards that formed the crib (plus the 'start' card). So the dealer has greater chances of scoring high, and deal alternates between the players.

The target is 121 points or more, although you can play a short version up to 61. Scoring continues during play, which ceases as soon as the target is reached. In terms of strategy, the non-dealer should aim to put combination-scoring cards in the crib. A good card to play first of all is the 4, since no card added to it would make fifteen. Keep your eye on the score as you can adapt your play to frustrate an opponent.

Variation
★ *FIVE CARD CRIBBAGE* In this, the original version of the game, the dealer has an even greater advantage. Five cards are dealt and two must be laid away, leaving three in each hand and four in the crib. Non-dealer starts with 3 points, a flush counts 3 in hand, 4 with the 'start', but can score 5 in the crib.

IMPERIAL

★ **OBJECTIVE:**   to win points by trick taking and point scoring.

Imperial is also known as Piquet with a Trump, and is played with a Piquet pack or a 32-card deck (standard deck with twos to sixes, inclusive, removed). Cards rank king, queen, jack, ace, ten, nine, eight, seven, and the king, queen, jack, ace and seven of trumps are honours.

For scoring, a pot of 12 white and nine red tokens is required. A red chip is worth six whites.

Hands of 12 cards are dealt three cards at a time, and the next card is turned up to denote trumps. Players then 'announce' or declare, their hands as in Piquet, with each player stating the number of cards in his longest suit, longest sequence, and for his highest set of three or more same-rank cards. Exceptions to Piquet are that:

a) Non-dealer scores for all equals;

b) Announcements commence with declarations of imperials, which are carte blanche (a hand with no court cards) and a sequence of king, queen, jack, ace, in one suit, or four kings, queens, jacks, aces or sevens. Sets of three do not count. The dealer can use the turned trump to complete a sequence of a kind, otherwise the card cannot be used. He then announces his point, and leads.

Before playing the lead, the dealer shows his imperials, and shows a superior point (the numerical total of the best suit in his hand, aces counting 11, picture cards 10, others their face value) or concedes an inferior one, in which case the opponent shows his point: all combinations scored must be exposed for inspection.

Imperials must be declared first, then his points, and the points must be announced before play commences.

The non-dealer leads and his opponent must follow suit or if he cannot, trump, otherwise he discards – but he must try to win the trick. Points are made by winning a trick containing a trump honour or honours. Tricks are displayed face up throughout the game and can be examined at any time.

During the declaring phase, a red chip is taken for every imperial the player declares, and whoever has the highest point takes one white chip. If the turned up trump is an honour, the dealer takes a white chip. Catching the jack and ace of trumps by leading the king or queen earns a red chip, and a white chip is taken for every honour won in a trick. If one player wins more tricks than the other, he takes a white chip for each trick in excess of his opponent's. Capot (all twelve tricks) scores two red chips. As soon as any player has six white chips he exchanges them for a red one, at which point his opponent must return any white chips he holds.

As soon as a player has won five red chips, he wins the game, whatever the stage of play.

JASS

★ *OBJECTIVE*:   to score points by melding and trick taking.

Each player is dealt nine cards (in threes) from the 36-card deck, made by stripping out all cards below the six, i.e. from five down. The next card is turned up to denote trumps, and the remainder becomes the stock. If a player holds the six of trumps, he may exchange it for the upturned card.

The rank of cards in no-trumps is ace (high), king, queen, jack, ten, nine, eight, seven, six, but in trumps it is jack, nine, ace, king, queen, ten, eight, seven, six.

The winner of each trick takes the top card from stock, his opponent the next. Melds can only be made one at a time by the winner of a trick, before he leads for the next.

Only certain melds are allowed, and these are listed here with their values:

Four jacks	200
Four aces, kings, queens or tens	100
A sequence of five (same suit)	100
A sequence of four (same suit)	50
A sequence of three (same suit)	20
King and queen of trumps	20

NB. For sequences the no-trumps ranking stands for all suits. Melds continue to form part of the hand and once scored can be played in tricks. Once broken up by having a card from it played, a meld remains on the table and can be scored again if another suitable card becomes available (this applies t͜ sequences where the top card may be played but a bottom card added).

There is no obligation to follow suit until stock is exhausted, after which players must try to win tricks, and from this point on, melds cannot be made. At the end of play, players count the cards of value in the tricks they have won. The values are:

Jack of trumps (jass)	20
Nine of trumps	14
Any ace	11
Any ten	10
Any king	4
Any queen	3
Other jacks	2

Winning the last trick earns another five points. If a player scores under 21, he loses 100 points overall. Winner is the first to 1,000, to be announced by a player who thinks he has achieved it. If he is wrong, he loses.

THE RANK OF CARDS IN TRUMPS

If this player wins the trick with his 9 of trumps, he can add the 10 to his meld on the table and make a new score.

KLOB (also known as KLABBERJASS)

★ *OBJECTIVE:*   to score points through melds and trick taking.

Klob uses a 32-card deck, formed by removing all cards ranked six and below. The rank of cards is ace (high) down to seven, except in the trump suit, when it becomes jack (high), nine, ace, ten, king, queen, eight, seven.

The first dealer is decided by whoever cuts the lowest card, and he deals six cards each, three at a time. The next card is turned up and placed in such a way that it is readily identifiable under the stock.

The aim is to be the first to score 300 or 500 points, as agreed, which is done by melding certain combinations; and scoring by taking tricks which contain certain high value cards.

Non-dealer has first say on what is trump. He may accept the suit of the turned up card as trumps. If not, he passes, and the dealer faces the same choice. If both pass, the cards are shuffled and redealt. Players have a third option, of saying 'Schmeiss' or 'Throw them in', an offer to start again. His opponent can accept and throw in his hand, or refuse. If this is the first round, the turned up card becomes trumps, if it is the second or later rounds, the player who called 'Schmeiss' names the trump suit.

After trumps are decided, three more cards each are dealt, and the bottom card from stock placed, turned up, on top of it. If a player holds the seven of trumps, he may exchange it for the card originally upturned as trump if he chooses.

Players now announce (or declare, without showing) their melds, or matched sets, to compete for scoring – for only one player may score a meld or melds. Melds can be a sequence of three, four or more same suit cards. A three-card meld is worth 20 points, one of four or more is valued at 50 points. Melds longer than four do not carry a higher value.

If the non-dealer has a meld he states its points value by calling either 'twenty' or 'fifty'. If the dealer has no melds or only some of lower value, he says 'good'. If he has a higher point value he replies 'No good' and shows and scores his meld. If he had a meld of the same value, he asks 'How high?', and his opponent must name the highest ranking card in his meld. The dealer responds with 'Same', 'Good' or 'No good' as appropriate.

Should both players have same value melds with equal top-ranking, no-trumps cards, the non-dealer scores. If one of the melds is a trump suit, it wins. If non-dealer has no melds, he says so and the dealer calls out the points value of his melds. All melds scored must be shown. Players may choose not to show certain melds simply to keep their hand secret. If a player has king and queen of trumps, this is a meld known as a bella, worth 20 points, and need not be declared until the game is completed, when it is added to the score.

Non-dealer plays first, and tricks are played for in the usual way – each player must try to win each trick and must follow suit or if not, trump if possible. After the nine tricks have been played, players calculate the point value of the cards gathered from the tricks they have won. Jack of trumps is worth 20 points, nine of trumps 14, any ace 11, any ten 10, any king 4, any queen 3, no-trump jacks 2. The winner of the final trick scores another 10. The maximum possible score from one hand is 156.

If the player who bid trumps has the higher total score (including melds) each player's score remains the same. If the non-bidder scores the same as or higher than his opponent, he earns both scores, and the bidder scores nought and is said to have 'gone bate'. First to 330 or 500 points (as agreed beforehand) wins, with the higher score winning if both players beat the target.

Variations

★ *BELOTTE* In this version, schmeiss is vale valse (waltz). Highest ranking melds are four of a kind, counting 200 for jacks, and 100 for nines, aces, tens, kings, or queens (in rank order). A five-card sequence is worth 50, four 40, and three 20. The player with the highest ranking group scores all his groups, while whoever has the highest ranking sequence scores all his sequences. If bidder does not score above his opponent, his score is nullified but not passed over to the other player.

★ *DARDA* This is played as Klob, except:

1) The rank of cards in trumps is queen, nine, ace, ten, king, jack, eight, seven, and the queen counts 20, the jack 2. No-trump rankings are ace, ten, king, queen, jack, nine, eight, seven. There is no schmeiss.

2) After trumps are named and the three extra cards have been dealt, the stock is turned face up, with only the top card showing. The seven of trumps may be exchanged for this card (eight of trumps if the seven was turned), and players can then exchange any card from their hands for the exposed card, provided it is a trump.

3) The bidder leads, and then any melds which are to be scored are announced, the trick played, and scoring completed.

4) The bidder wins if his opponent has a lower score, and scores 1 if he has up to 100 points, 2 for 100–149, 3 for 150–199, and 4 for 200 or more. Game is 10 points.

5) If four of a kind are held by either player, there is no play. The highest four of a kind wins, scoring 4 for queens, 3 for nines, 2 for other cards.

PINOCHLE

★ **OBJECTIVE:**   to win cards in tricks, and to form certain melds.

For this popular game, derived from Bezique, you need an unusually formed deck of 48 cards, made from two decks with all cards from eight downward removed, leaving two of each card from ace to nine.

The aim is to win tricks containing scoring cards, and to meld certain combinations of cards. The ranking order and points value is:

Ace	11
Ten	10
King	4
Queen	3
Jack	2
Nine	zero

Whoever wins the last trick scores 10 points. Values of melds are:

Ace, 10, king, queen, jack of trumps	150
Four aces, one of each suit (no pairs)	100
Four kings, one of each suit (no pairs)	80
Four queens, one of each suit (no pairs)	60
Four jacks, one of each suit (no pairs)	40
Pinochle (queen of spades, jack of diamonds)	40
King and queen of trumps (royal marriage)	40
King and queen of other suits (common marriage)	20
Dix (nine of trumps)	10

Bundles of three cards are dealt until there are two hands of 12, the next card being turned up (the 'upcard') to indicate trumps, and the rest of the pack faced downwards as the stock. Non-dealer leads first, and tricks are played for with no obligation to follow suit. If identical cards are played, the one led wins. After each trick the winner places the won cards face down before him, then his opponent draws a card from stock to keep their hands at 12 cards.

Melds can only be made after winning a trick and drawing from stock. Only one meld is allowed per turn, and it is scored immediately. At least one card in it must be taken from the hand (cards can be moved around once on the table to form higher scoring melds). A card can only be used once in each meld, and once in each sequence or matching rank group per player. However, a card can be used twice provided it is in different types of melds. So a player with four queens can score the meld, then at a later turn add a king to make a marriage.

Melded cards are still part of the hand, and can be played in tricks. A player holding dix (nine of trumps) can meld it when he wins a trick, or exchange it for the upcard, and still score 10.

RANKING ORDER IN PINOCHLE

MELD

HAND

Hearts are trumps. If this player picks up the Ace of Hearts, he can use it with the hearts in his hand and the heart from his meld to form a new meld worth 150 points.

The winner of the 12th trick makes his meld and draws the last card from stock, showing it to his opponent, who takes the upcard. For these final tricks played with a diminishing hand, with no play allowed from the melds, players should follow suit if they can, and trump if they cannot.

Each player will have a running total of declared melds, to which is now added points for cards won in tricks, and 10 points for winning the last trick. Points of 7, 8 and 9 are scored as 10. Six and below is ignored. The scores for each round should add up to 250 points, and the usual winning target is 1,000. If a player believes he has reached this target during play, he declares it and scoring begins. If he is right, he wins, if not, he loses – an expensive mistake! If neither announces he is over 1,000 and both find they have passed this total, another 250 points is added to the target.

The strategy of Pinochle is quite complicated, and is based on a need to make melds early on, while building up a strong hand for the second phase of play. There may be times when a player uses high cards to win tricks simply to stop his opponent from melding, and others when he leads from his long suit simply to balance his hand. As usual in complicated card games, a good memory for cards played helps – but this is tricky in a game like Pinochle when every card has a twin!

PIQUET

★ *OBJECTIVE:*   to build scoring combinations and a trick winning hand.

This game, dating back to 15th century France, requires a 32-card deck – two packs are usually used alternately. The rank of cards is ace (high), king, queen, jack, ten, nine, eight, seven. Each player receives 12 cards, dealt in pairs. The remaining eight cards are spread face down on the table to form the stock.

The non-dealer examines his hand and must discard between one and five cards, replacing them from the stock. The dealer is allowed to discard the same number of cards, and is entitled to take all of the stock left by his opponent. He does not have to take any cards from the stock. Any remaining cards are turned up or left face down at his discretion.

The purpose of discarding is to form scoring combinations as follows:

Carte blanche: A hand with no king, queen or jack. If dealt a carte blanche, the player may expose it before his discard and scores 10 points.

Point: The greatest number of cards in any suit scores for point as many cards as are held. Between two holdings of the same length, the value of the cards (ace is 11, picture cards and tens 10, others as their face value) comes into play. If the points are still tied, neither player scores.

Sequence: A sequence of three consecutive value cards in the same suit (tierce) counts 3 points. Four in sequence scores 4, and five or more counts for 10 plus the number of cards. Only the player holding the highest sequence can score, and he can then score for all additional sequences held. Any sequence is higher than one of lesser length, and if two are of equal length, the one headed by the higher card scores. If the players tie in this category, neither scores for sequence.

Sets: Three or four cards of the same rank, higher than nine, form a set. The player holding the highest set scores it and any other sets he holds. Four of a kind, counting 14, is higher than three of a kind, counting 3. In the event of equal number sets being held, the higher in rank of cards scores.

Once the discarding is completed, and starting with the non-dealer, players verbally declare their holdings to determine in order the scores for point, sequence and sets. The player who does not score in a category need not give any more information than is necessary to establish his opponent's superiority.

Thus, if the non-dealer starts by saying 'four', for the longest length of a suit, the dealer will respond with either 'good', if he has no longer suit, or 'five' if he has five cards in a suit. If he has four cards of the same suit too, he says 'how much?', asking for the points value of his opponent's longest suit.

Declaring continues through each category, and although a player is not obliged to declare any combination, he cannot later change his mind. If requested, a player must show any combinations for which he has scored, although this is usually unnecessary. This stage of the game allows for the accumulation of a great deal of information about the opponent's hand.

Non-dealer then leads for the first trick, which will be won by the higher card of the suit led. One point is scored by each card he leads higher than a nine, and if he beats an opponent's lead with a card higher than nine. A variation is to simply award one point for each trick won. The last trick carries an extra point for the winner.

Each player announces the running total of his score as play continues, including the initial count for combinations.

The winner of seven or more tricks scores 10. If tricks are split six all, neither scores. Winning the whole dozen tricks scores 40 (with no extra score for the final trick). If a player reaches 30 or more in declarations, before his opponent scores at all or a card has been played, he scores 60 for repique. If this score is reached without answer during play, he adds 30 for pique. Once all tricks are played, the scores are noted.

There are three variations on how the winner of the game is decided:

1. Piquet au Cent. A total score of 100 or more wins,

with settlement made on the difference between the final scores. If the loser failed to reach 50 points, this difference is doubled. The last deal of the game is played out with no running count of scores kept.

2. Rubicon Piquet. The game is run over six deals. The player with the highest cumulative score wins the difference of the totals, plus 100 for game, provided the loser reached at least 100. If not, he is rubiconed, and the winner scores the sum of both totals plus 100 for game. This is enforced even if the winner failed to reach 100 as well.

3. Club Piquet. The game is run over four deals, with the scores of the first and last deal doubled.

PITCH

★ **OBJECTIVE:**   to score points by capturing certain cards.

There are a number of versions of Pitch.

AUCTION PITCH, (or SET-BACK)

Each player is dealt three cards at a time until each has a hand of six.

The object of the game is to become the first player to score 11 points (or 7, 9, 10 or 21, as agreed by the players).

Points are counted after the game has been played, and are:

High: One point for the original player holding the highest trump of either hand.

Low: One point for the original player holding the lowest trump showing during the play of the hand.

Jack: One point to the player who wins the jack of trumps during play, assuming it comes into play.

Game: One point to the player who wins most points in tricks, cards valued as ace 4, king 3, queen 2, jack 1, ten 10.

Starting with the non-dealer, each player may bid 1, 2, 3, o4 4, or pass. Each bid must be higher than the last. If both players pass, the pack is shuffled and cards are dealt again.

The highest bidder leads the first trick, his card also indicating trumps. Players must either follow suit or trump, or if they can do neither, discard. The winner of each trick leads for the next, and this continues until all six cards are played.

Scoring: Points values are described above. If a player fails to score what he bid for, the full total of what he bid is deducted from his score. Minus scores are allowed.

The winner is the first to an agreed number of points. If both players reach the total, the top bidder of the last hand wins. In terms of strategy at Auction Pitch, the dealer bids last, and should take risks to win the bidding. Holding three cards of one suit merits a bid of one, as does holding the jack. Both very high and very low value cards strengthen the hand, but remember if players can trump they do not have to follow suit – so an ace is not necessarily a winner.

Variations

★ *SMUDGE* In Smudge, winning all four points in one hand constitutes a smudge, and wins the game immediately, regardless of previous scoring. In another variant, if you achieve a smudge but have a minus score, you do not win but your score becomes four.

★ *JOKER PITCH* This is Auction Pitch with a joker, which ranks as the lowest trump, but only scores if it is used to win a trick. The lowest trump score remains as before.

★ *LOW PITCH* Low can only be scored by the player winning a trick with it.

★ *RACEHORSE PITCH* Played with a 32-card deck, ace high to seven low. Points are scored for high, low, jack, and game, in that order.

★ *PEDRO* Pedro is a whole group of Auction Pitch variants.

Pedro: The five of trumps is called Pedro, and is worth 5 points. The target is to win 21 points.

Pedro Sancho: In addition to the five, the nine of trumps (Sancho) has a value of nine points. Scoring is: high, low, jack, ten of trumps (which takes the place of game), Pedro, and Sancho. First to 50 points is the winner.

Dom Pedro or Snoozer: Joker Pitch combined with Pedro Sancho. The three of trumps (Dom) is worth 3 points when taken in play. The Joker (Snoozer) is worth 15 points to the taker. Dom counts after the ten, Snoozer after Sancho. Snoozer ranks below the two in trumps, but is not scored as low. First to 100 points wins.

POKINO

★ *OBJECTIVE:*   to build a winning hand.

This gambling game is played in two stages: Five Card Draw Poker, then the playing out of tricks.

Five cards each are dealt, and starting with the non-dealer, players can discard and draw up to three cards at the same time from stock to improve the hand. This process can be repeated, but the penalty score for every trick lost in the next stage doubles with each set of discard and draws. The dealer incurs no penalty for his first draw of up to three cards.

His opponent then leads, and the tricks are played out, with highest card winning, regardless of suit. If both cards are of the same value, the first led wins. After each trick players retrieve their cards, turning them up if the trick was won, down if lost. A player can lead a pair (two of a kind), and his opponent can only win by playing a larger pair, although he can discard any cards he wishes if he chooses.

Pokino is scored rather like Bridge, in columns divided by a line. Trick scores go below the line, bonuses and honours go above the line. Each won trick is worth a point (or two if the opponent is doubled, etc). After the final trick, players show their (original Poker hands, the winning Poker hand scoring honours as shown in the table below.

If a player wins all five tricks (a sweep) he gets a 250-point bonus. Winning a game equals 20 points below the line, and the player making game receives a 100 point bonus above the line, with all partial trick scores of his opponent below the line cancelled. If the same player wins his second game, he gets a 100-point bonus plus 750 provided his opponent has not won a game, 500 if he has.

Table of honours:

Pair	50
Two pairs	100
Three of a kind	200
Straight	300
Flush	400
Full house	500
Four of a kind	600
Straight flush	750
Royal flush	1,000

SIXTY SIX

★ **OBJECTIVE:**   to score by making melds and capturing key cards.

This is played with 24 cards (ace to nine of each suit), with ranks as follows: ace (high), ten, king, queen, jack, nine (low). Most of the scoring is through declaring a specific kind of meld: a king and queen pair.

Six cards each are dealt, three at a time, with the next card turned up, to decide trumps, and left beside the stock.

The non-dealer leads a card. Players do not have to follow suit (including trumps), and can trump at will. A trick is won by the highest card of the suit led, unless a trump is played. Winner of each trick places it face down in front of him, then draws the top card from stock, and after his opponent has taken the next, leads for the next trick.

After he has won at least one trick and it is his turn to play, the player holding the nine of trumps may exchange it for the turned up trump card. But if the nine of trumps happens to be the last card of the stock, it may not be exchanged, and his opponent gets the trump card.

A player who has won at least one trick and is to lead may meld a marriage in his hand (the king and queen of the same suit) by showing the pair and leading one of them. The non-dealer may declare such a marriage on his first lead, and score it when he wins a trick. Marriages can only be announced in leading them, unless they are going to take a player's score to 66 or over. When the stock is gone, a player must follow suit if he can, but is not required to win a trick.

Either player who is about to lead may announce the game is now 'closed'. He may do this before or after drawing a card, but if he has drawn, so can his opponent. Closing is shown by turning over the trump card, and after this no cards can be drawn from stock.

Play continues until both hands are played out, and the last trick does not score 10.

Scoring is as follows:

Marriage in trumps (king and queen announced)	40
Marriage in any other suits (announced)	20
Each ace taken in on tricks	11
Each ten taken in on tricks	10
Each king taken in on tricks	4
Each queen taken in on tricks	3
Each jack taken in on tricks	2
Winning last trick	10

The player who reaches 66 points first scores one game point. If he reaches this before his opponent has 33, he scores two game points. If his opponent has failed to get a trick at all, he scores three game points. If neither scores 66, or each reaches 66 or more without announcing it, neither gets the game point, which is added to the score of the winner of the next hand.

If a player closing gets 66 or more, he scores the same as if the game had been played out. If he fails, his opponent gets two points. If a player closes before his opponent has taken a trick, but still fails to score 66, the opponent gets 3 points. Play stops the moment either player announces his score is 66 or more. The game ends when one player has scored seven game points.

Variation

★ *GAIGEL* This can be played by two to eight players, when it is played as a partnership. A 48-card deck is used, made up with two 52-card decks with all cards except sevens between two and nine inclusive removed. Cards are ranked ace, ten, king, queen, jack, seven. If two identical cards are led, the one played first is ranked highest.

Each player receives five cards, dealt as three and then two. The next card is turned up to show trumps, and the remainder are left face down on the table.

Scoring is as follows:

Common marriage (king and queen of plain suit)	20
Double common marriage (pairs of the above)	40
Royal marriage (king and queen of trumps)	40
Double royal marriage (pairs of the above)	80
Any five sevens, drawn or held at one time	101
Each ace taken in on tricks	11
Each ten taken in on tricks	10
Each king taken in on tricks	4
Each queen taken in on tricks	3
Each jack taken in on tricks	2

Non-dealer leads, and players are not compelled to follow suit, and winners are highest card of suit led or highest trump. Tricks are stored face down in front of their winner.

The winner of each trick then takes the top card from stock, his opponent the next. After winning a trick, and before drawing from the stock, a player may declare one marriage, showing it to his opponent. Two single marriages cannot be declared in the same suit during any hand, and the second scores nothing.

After he takes a trick and before drawing from stock, a player holding a seven of trumps (dix), may exchange it for the turned-up trump card, scoring 10 points. The holder of the other seven of trumps shows it after winning a trick, and also scores 10.

When all cards are drawn from stock, melding ceases, and players must follow suit, and must try to win the trick in the suit led or by a trump. Failure to do either of these when possible forfeits the game.

Both players keep a mental count of points made

by cards taken in tricks and are not permitted to record them. Melds are entered on a score sheet as they are made. When a player believes he has reached 101 points, he stops playing and knocks on the table. If he is wrong, he forfeits the game. Only the last trick played can be examined at this point, and if a claim of game is questioned, the disputed player's tricks are turned over and counted. In counting for going out, marriages take precedence over all other scores. Each game won scores one point, and the winner is the first to seven.

A gaigel, or bonus, is awarded for double game (two game points) and scores 202 points. It can be achieved as follows:

Scoring 101 before your opponent has won a trick.
Holding five sevens in a hand, before opponents have won a trick.
When an opponent claims to be out, and is wrong.
When the opponents play again after reaching 101.
When opponents refuse the privilege of counting the current trick again, or mix the cards before the count is agreed.
When an error is claimed and the claim is baseless.

SPITE AND MALICE

★ *OBJECTIVE:*   to get rid of your pay-off pile.

This is an excellent two-handed solitaire game in which either player has chances of winning right up to the last card. Two standard decks with differing backs plus four jokers are required, and ace counts low.

One deck, without the jokers, is split in half, and these 26 cards each will form the player's pay-off piles. Each selects a pile and turns over the the top card. Whoever has the higher card is the lead player, as each player will play in turn. If both are of the same rank, start again.

The second deck, with the four jokers, is shuffled by the non-lead player, who deals hands of five to them both, the remainder being put in the middle of the table as stock.

As it becomes available, each ace must be played immediately to form a new centre stack, and any available twos must be added, then threes, and so on, in ascending order, regardless of suit. Each player is allowed four side stacks, which act as discard piles. A player can only add to his own side stacks, and only from his hand. Side stacks can start at any value but must be built downward, regardless of suit, or with like cards (e.g. jack on jack).

To start play, the top card in the pay-off pile must be played to the centre, and when it is, the next card in the pay-off pile is turned up. Cards from the hand, or the top of any of the side stacks, can be played to the centre piles as and when this is possible.

At the start of each turn, the player draws cards from stock to give him a hand of five. Only one card from the hand per turn can be played to a side stack, and this signifies the end of a player's turn, so should always be left as the last play, after making plays to the centre stack. Cards cannot be moved between side stacks, or to fill a place. Players can end their turn at any point by saying they do not wish to play.

Jokers are wild and can take the place of any card except an ace. If a joker comes to the top of a pay-off or side stack, it can be played to the centre. When any centre stack is built up as far as the king, it is shuffled back into stock.

First player to empty his pay-off pile wins, his score being one point for each card left in his opponent's pay-off pile. If both players have cards left but cannot make a play, the winner is the one who has fewer cards in his pile, and his score is the difference between the two. Cards in the pay-off pile cannot be counted during play.

SPOIL FIVE

★ **OBJECTIVE:**   to win three or five tricks.

Ranking of cards is somewhat unusual in the gambling game of Spoil Five. In a trump suit, the five counts highest, followed by the jack. Whatever the trump suit, the ace of hearts is always the third highest trump. In plain suits, the ace counts low in hearts and diamonds, and after the jack in clubs and spades.

Each player puts a token into the pot, and first to be dealt a jack is dealer. Hands of five are dealt in twos and threes, and the next card turned up represents trumps. If it is an ace, the dealer can immediately pick it up and discard. If his opponent holds the ace of trumps, he passes his discard face down to dealer in exchange for the turned-up card. If the dealer holds the ace, he discards under the stock on his turn and picks up the turned-up card.

The aim of the game is to win three and if possible five tricks, and if not, prevent your opponent doing so. Players must either follow suit or trump if they can, unless they hold the 5 or jack of trumps or the ace of hearts, which they are only forced to play if a higher trump has been led. (You will begin to see how complicated this ranking structure is!)

If no-one wins three tricks the game is 'spoiled', and the new dealer puts a token in the pool and deals for the next hand. Winning three tricks wins the pool. However, if these are the first three tricks, the player can either throw-in his cards or say he will 'jink it', meaning he expects to win the next two tricks. If he fails, the pool stands for the next game.

Spoil Five is a game of stealth in which the object is quite often to sabotage your opponent's chances of winning three tricks, which, given the ranking of cards and the rules of trumping, is perfectly possible.

Variation

★ *FORTY FIVE* This variation of Spoil Five is scored by points. The player taking three or four tricks scores 5, and five tricks score 10. Alternatively, every single trick counts, for winner and loser, and one is then deducted from the other. So three tricks scores 15 minus 10 = 5. Four tricks score 15, and five tricks score 25. Game is 45 points. Sometimes this figure for game is 25.

THIRTY FIVE

★ *OBJECTIVE:* to have a hand worth 35 or more points in one suit.

In this gambling game the court cards (kings, queens, jacks) count 10 points, aces count 1, and all other cards count their face value. A central pot with betting units is required.

The banker deals three hands of four – one each and one on the table, called the 'buy'. Then a further five cards are dealt to both players, so they have hands of nine cards. The 22 cards now in play are the only active cards. Starting with the non-banker, players bid for the 'buy' – the chance to discard four cards in exchange for the four on the table. Bidding continues until one player drops out.

Once the winning bidder has his new hand, he announces his points and if he has 35 points or more, removes his bid value from the pot. If it was higher than the amount in the pot, he simply takes as much as there is. If he scores 34 or less, he puts his bid into the pot.

If a player scores 35 before the bidding stage, he announces it and wins the pot. If both players achieve this, they share the pot.

INDEX